THE STUDENT PRAYERBOOK

See pages 239 and 240 for complete list of HADDAM HOUSE books published to date.

THE STUDENT
PRAYERBOOK

Edited and written by a Haddam House committee under the chairmanship of John Oliver Nelson for personal and group devotion

---

A Haddam House Book

ASSOCIATION PRESS • NEW YORK

Fifth Printing, February, 1960

Printed in the United States of America
American Book–Stratford Press, Inc., New York

CONTENTS

[v]

PART IV
GENERAL PRAYERS

PART V
APPENDIX

To Those Who Use This Book

More harm than good will be done by this little volume if it keeps young people from praying their own prayers because they rely on printed suggestions. But as this generation asks with new urgency, "Teach us to pray," the forms given here prompt us by gathering up some of the richness of devotion expressed by others. It is intended for the seat-rack in many a small chapel, for student services in conference grove or prayer circle, and most of all for the study table and the bedside where private devotion is likely to be kept.

For private prayer, not only the first section for morning and evening worship, but all the other prayers as well, may be useful. It helps to choose in advance a progression, noting down the numbers, then turning to them during the period of actual meditation without the interruption of choosing and finding. Litanies prayed through by an individual can be as suggestive as other forms. Concentrate in silence before reading the printed words, allowing the silt of your spirit to settle so that you may be clear to know your own thoughts and phrases after the reading.

For corporate use, any selection of single prayers may be read in unison or by a leader. A few use "I" instead of "we," but this is readily assimilated in group worship. Prayers which provide frequent stops for breathing are better for group reading than others. With litanies, the traditional usage is for the leader to read the verse, the group then joining in the italicized response. If the whole group does not have copies of the book, the leader announces in advance the responsive phrase or phrases to be said from memory by the others, he himself joining in the responses. However, it is often more meaningful to divide the group (as by an aisle) in halves: one half reads the verse with its italicized affirmation added, the other half then following with the next verse with italicized affirmation, and so on, turn about. This lessens the impression that the leader alone is offering creative prayer, the others merely adding an assent. By either usage, a regular rhythm and pace of reading should be kept.

Elements of worship for any gathering of Christians, led with hymns, Scripture, prayer, and silence, are generally agreed to be these:

> *Adoration*—exaltation and praise of God
> *Confession*—acknowledgment of our unworthiness
> *Thanksgiving*—gratitude for all blessings
> *Intercession*—God's will asked for others
> *Petition*—prayer for our own wants and needs

Prayers for each step of this pattern (ACTIP, by its initial letters) are to be found in the various sections of this book. It is hoped that leaders will seek to write their own prayers, or better, speak them from the basis of a previously made outline.

Omissions Many hymns are inspiring prayers, but none has been given here because they are readily accessible elsewhere. Creedal statements are omitted for the same reason, as also for the reason that the approach sought here is ecumenical, seeking to serve all evangelical and Protestant communions. The principle that God is "ever more ready to hear than we are to pray," has prompted prayerful excising of terms such as *beseech* and *implore* as often as possible, these seeming to imply that we must plead with God to hear us. Most of the prayers conclude with indication that we approach God through Christ; but not all, for it is assumed that *all* our prayer is in Christ. At the same time, we are aware that some students may find prayer addressed to Christ himself unaccustomed: here with all the Christian generations we approach him as the revelation of God himself, our devotion being addressed to God known in Christ.

This is the first book of its kind for students and other young people in this country. The process by which it came into being and the Committee which worked on it, are noted on page 221. It is sent out with the Committee's own prayer that even these printed suggestions will help rekindle the personal and corporate worship of God among students.

PART I. DEVOTIONS FOR FOURTEEN DAYS—MORNING AND EVENING

FIRST DAY'S DEVOTION
Morning

---

1 O Lord, who makest all things new, yet abidest forever, grant us so to pass through this coming day with faithful hearts that we may spend each hour in thy service, and in all things do thy loving will, through Christ our Lord. *Amen*

Read: *Psalm 96   Sing unto the Lord*

O God, before the wonder and beauty of nature, and the noble heights of the human spirit, we stand in awe. We are deeply conscious that we have marred life's fair prospects by our lack of appreciation, our feverish haste, and our moral weakness. Forgive us, O God, and make us henceforth more true to thee, in Christ. *Amen*

O God, we thank thee for this universe, our great home; for its vastness and its riches, and for the manifoldness of the life which teems upon it and of which we are part. We praise thee for the arching sky and the blessed winds, for the driving clouds and the constellations on high. We praise thee for the salt sea and the running water, for the everlasting hills, for the trees, and for the grass under our feet. We thank thee for our senses by which we can see the splendor of the morning, and hear the jubilant songs of love, and smell the breath of the springtime. Grant us, we pray thee, a heart wide open to all this joy and beauty, and save our souls from being so steeped in care or so darkened by passion that we pass heedless and unseeing when even the thornbush by the wayside is aflame with thy glory. When our use of this world is over and we make room for others, may we not leave anything ravished by our greed or spoiled by our ignorance; but may we hand on our common heritage fairer and sweeter through our use of it. *Amen*

Grant, Lord, that what we have said with our lips we may believe in our hearts and practice in our lives; and of thy mercy keep us faithful unto the end. *Amen*

[2]

FIRST DAY'S DEVOTION
Evening

---

2 Accept the work of this day, O Lord, as we lay it at thy feet. Thou knowest its imperfections, and we know. Accept every right intention however brokenly fulfilled; but grant that before our life is done, we may under thy teaching become true master workmen, who know the art of a just and valiant life. *Amen*

Read: *Isaiah 40:1-11, 28-31 Walk and faint not*

Draw our affections, Lord, up to the heights where thou dwellest, that our hearts being set not on things seen but on things unseen, our lives may be shaped according to thy pattern and filled with the vision of thy beauty, through Christ our Lord. *Amen*

Give me sound and refreshing sleep:
Give me safety from all perils:
Give me in my sleep freedom from restless dreams:
Give me control of my thoughts, if I should lie awake:
Give me wisdom to remember that the night was made
      for sleeping, and not for the harboring of anxious
      or fretful or shameful thoughts.

From all the blunders and follies of the day; from its wandering desires and its unjust judgments; from any sense of grievance or any word of blame which has blotted the fair hours; good Lord, deliver us. May the meaning of life shine through the gathering dusk like the watching stars. Lift our minds to the vision of the permanent; rescue our wills from the illusion of the day's gain or loss; that the pressure of routine may not crush the life of the spirit, or the gain of the world become the loss of the soul. May we rest tonight in the protecting shadow of thy love, and wake with new courage and hope to fulfill the duties of another day, through Christ. *Amen*

SECOND DAY'S DEVOTION
Morning

3 We give thee hearty thanks for the rest of this past night, and for the gift of a new day, with its opportunities of pleasing thee. Grant that we may so pass its hours in the perfect freedom of thy service, that at eventide we may again give thanks unto thee, through Jesus Christ our Lord. *Amen*

Read: *Ephesians 6:10-24   The whole armor of God*

Give unto us, O God, the girdle, the helmet, the breast-plate, the shield, the sandals, the sword—above all things, prayer. Grant unto us the power and opportunity of well-doing, that before the day is gone we may have wrought at least somewhat, whose good fruit may remain; that we may behold thy presence in righteousness, and be satisfied with thy glory, for Christ's sake. *Amen*

O God, who hast called us to thy service, show us thy purpose for our lives; though it be hard, make us long to follow it; and give us courage to persevere till, at the last, we reach the goal which thou hast set for us. *Amen*

O God, thou knowest the duties that lie ahead of us, the dangers that confront us, the weaknesses that most easily beset us. In the valiant spirit of Jesus we would dedicate to thee our studies, our friendships, our family relationships, our recreation, our leisure, our decisions, and our future, that so in thought and word and deed we may glorify thy Name, by the power of Jesus Christ, our Lord. *Amen*

Teach us, good Lord, to serve thee as thou deservest; to give and not to count the cost; to fight and not to heed the wounds; to toil and not to seek for rest; to labor and not to ask for any reward, save that of knowing that we do thy will, through Jesus Christ our Lord. *Amen*

[4]

SECOND DAY'S DEVOTION
Evening

---

4 O God, pardon all that we have done in willful or thoughtless disregard of thy honor, and of our neighbor's good. If we have this day by word or deed made life harder for any of our brethren, or faith in goodness less easy, forgive us, gracious Father, and in thy mercy undo the wrongs we have done. *Amen*

Read: *Psalm 27 Teach me thy way, O Lord*

We are inwardly led, our Father, to seek thee daily. There is that within us that goes out after thee, and will not be satisfied unless we find thee. We thank thee that wherever and whensoever we seek thee we may find thee. We are comforted with the assurance that whatsoever we do thou art with us; whether we wake or sleep, whether we work or play, whether we meditate or pray, thou art near. Wheresoever we are or whatsoever we do, make us conscious of thy presence to sustain, to comfort, to rebuke, to chasten. Satisfy us, O God, with an ever-growing consciousness that thou art over us, that thou art round about us, that thou art within us. *Amen*

O thou eternal God, in whom we live and move and have our being, how may we utter our need of thee? Our minds need thee to give them poise. Our wills need thee to give them strength. Our hearts need thee to give them peace. We need thee as we labor for a better world, for great are the odds against which we must contend. Very urgent is our need of thee if we are to face persistent evil with hopeful determination. O thou who understandest us better than we do ourselves, grant unto us a healing, heartening consciousness of thy presence. *Amen*

Lord, temper with tranquillity our manifold activity; that we may do our work for thee with very great simplicity. *Amen*

[5]

THIRD DAY'S DEVOTION
Morning

---

5 O God, we praise thee, that through thy Son, Jesus Christ, thou hast transfigured the commonplaces of life with the light of an eternal adventure. We acknowledge that we have not been able to see life as a calling, and that our endeavors are sometimes fruitless because ungoverned by any settled aim. We would be lifted out of our drifting confusion by the dictates of some settled purpose that cometh from thee. *Amen*

Read: *Ephesians 2:11-22 Christ the Cornerstone*

Grant, O Lord, that the remembrance of the blessed life that once was lived out on this common earth, under these ordinary skies, may remain with me in all the tasks and duties of this day. Let me remember:
His eagerness, not to be ministered unto, but to minister;
His sympathy with suffering of every kind;
His bravery in face of his own suffering;
His meekness of bearing, so that when reviled, he reviled not again;
His steadiness of purpose in keeping to his appointed task;
His simplicity;
His self-discipline;
His serenity of spirit;
His complete reliance upon thee, his Father in heaven.
And in each of these ways give me grace to follow in his footsteps. *Amen*

O God, who art the giver of every good and perfect gift, for the outpoured life of Jesus Christ we thank thee. So often have we sought to avoid him, yet unfailingly has he followed us and this day comes knocking at our doors. Make us sensitive to the ways by which he would draw us to thee, that we may go out from this place to our work among men as those who know whom they serve, even Jesus Christ our Lord. *Amen*

THIRD DAY'S DEVOTION
Evening

---

6 God be in my head and in my understanding; God be in my eyes and in my looking; God be in my mouth and in my speaking; God be in my heart and in my thinking; God be at mine end and at my departing. *Amen*

Read: *John 15:1-17   The true vine*

O God, who hast set the solitary in families, who dost join man to man in friendship, and who dost kindle the hearts of nations to draw near to one another, grant us the gift of understanding. Make us sensitive to all troubled, lonely, disappointed persons. Make us sympathetic with all who are bereaved, frustrated, and ill. Make us eager to bear the burdens of the unemployed, the poor, and the homeless, people of all races and classes. Teach us to bless those who curse us, to pray for those who spitefully use us, and to forgive those who speak ill of us, or reject and pass proudly by. Take our spirits to those deep wellsprings of life eternal, where Jesus met thee face to face. Leave us ill-satisfied till thy love flows through us, and no barrier of our own mars the fulfillment of thine eternal purpose in us. *Amen*

Our Father, we thank thee for all the friendly folk who have come into our life this day. We send them now our evening thoughts of love through thee. Above all, we thank thee for those who share our higher life, the comrades of our better self, in whose companionship we break the mystic bread of life and feel the glow of thy wonderful presence. Into thy keeping we commit our friends, and pray that we may never lose their love by losing thee. *Amen*

Lighten our darkness, we beseech thee, O Lord, and by thy great mercy defend us from all perils and dangers of this night: for the love of thy only Son, our Savior Jesus Christ. *Amen*

[7]

FOURTH DAY'S DEVOTION
Morning

---

7 Grant us, O Lord, to pass thy day without stumbling and without stain, that reaching the eventide victorious over all temptation we may praise thee, the eternal God, who art blessed and dost govern all things, world without end. *Amen*

Read: *Ezekiel 18:1-9   Individual responsibility*

Father, as a new day comes to bring its unmarred opportunity, help me to use it better than I used yesterday. While there is yet time, I would remember the special temptations which have overcome me before, and can overcome me again unless I am better armed against them. I have been ashamed too late of the failure against which I ought to have been on guard. I have spoken harshly when I should have put a bit upon a hasty and bitter tongue; I have been so intent on my own way that I have turned others aside from the ways in which they might have walked more happily; I have been too preoccupied to be understanding and to be kind.

I do not ask that these faults may be forgiven now. I would not have the sharpness of my remembrance of them dulled. I ask rather that I may be made more thoughtful and more vigilant, so that when this day ends there may be less for which I need to be forgiven and more for which I may be glad; because I shall have tried to let the goodness of God express itself through my obedient mind and heart and will, through Christ. *Amen*

O God, lift us out of private-mindedness and give us public souls to work for thy kingdom, by daily creating that atmosphere of a happy temper and generous heart which alone can bring the perfect peace which has been won and offered to us, through our Lord Jesus Christ. *Amen*

FOURTH DAY'S DEVOTION
Evening

---

8 Heavenly Father, recall to our minds thy great good-ness. Enkindle our hearts with love. Make us willing and bold to draw near to thee in prayer, through Jesus Christ our Lord. *Amen*

Read: *Psalm 63 Thee will I seek*

Give me tonight, dear Father, a deeper sense of gratitude to thee for all thy mercies. Thy goodness to me has been wonderful. At no moment of the day have I lacked thy gracious care. At no moment of the day have I been called upon to stand in my own strength alone. When I was too busy with my petty concerns to remember thee, thou with a universe to govern wast not too busy to remember me. *Amen*

O God, who never sleepest and art never weary, have mercy upon those who watch tonight:
On those who command, that they may be strengthened with counsel;
On the sick, that they may obtain rest;
On the fainthearted, lest they forget thee;
On the dying, that they may find peace;
On the sinful, that they may turn again to thee.
Save us by thy mercy, O good Lord. *Amen*

O God our Father, in all our asking and seeking, we have forgotten to pause and wait for One whose quest is greater than our own, and who can be answered only when we give ourselves. Still the tumult of our hurried lives, and let us for a little space halt our search, and wait for thine, in quietness and silence. *Amen*

Abide with us, O searching and chastening Spirit of the living God, for it is evening and the day is far spent. Let the shadow of thy presence shelter us from the haste and fret of the day, and the sense of thy guidance give us tranquillity and rest. *Amen*

[9]

FIFTH DAY'S DEVOTION
Morning

9 Give us grace, we pray thee, O God, to greet the new day with expectant minds and obedient wills; and, in thy mercy, show us from hour to hour, among the cares and duties which await us, the way to go and the truth to trust and the life to lead. *Amen*

Read: *Isaiah 6:1-8   Here am I—send me*

Lord, who didst bid thy seraph purge the prophet's lips with fire from off the altar, that so he might be free to preach thy word unto the people, whether they would hear or whether they would forbear; give us, thy people, pure and wise hearts, that we may desire to go whither thou dost send us, and to do that which thou dost will, in the power of him through whom we do all things, even thy Son, Jesus Christ our Lord. *Amen*

O Eternal God, who committest to us the swift and solemn trust of life; since we know not what a day may bring forth, but only that the hour for serving thee is always present, may we wake to the instant claims of thy holy will, not waiting for tomorrow, but yielding today. Lay to rest, by the persuasion of thy Holy Spirit, the resistance of our passion, indolence, or fear. Consecrate with thy presence the way our feet may go, and the humblest work will shine, and the roughest places be made plain. Lift us above unrighteous anger and mistrust into faith and hope and charity by a simple and steadfast reliance on thy pure will. In all things draw us to the mind of Christ, that we may more fully serve thee. *Amen*

O Lord, quicken in us the spirit of courage that we may go forth with hopeful minds to the duties and conditions of this day, confident that with thy help we can fashion something good out of whatever material the day will provide, for thy name's sake. *Amen*

[10]

FIFTH DAY'S DEVOTION
Evening

---

10 Grant, O Lord, that against the confusion of false choices, and the restlessness of our unsure desires, we may know that in thy will is our peace, through Jesus Christ our Lord. *Amen*

Read: *Psalm 51   Have mercy, O God*

O Lord, in whose hands are life and death, by whose power I am sustained, and by whose mercy I am spared, look down upon me with compassion. Forgive me that I have this day neglected the duty which thou hast assigned to it, and suffered the hours, of which I must give account, to pass away without any endeavor to accomplish thy will, or to promote my own salvation. Make me to remember, O God, that every day is thy gift, and ought to be used according to thy command. Grant me, therefore, so to repent of my negligence that I may obtain mercy from thee, and pass the time which thou shalt yet allow me, in diligent performance of thy commands, through Jesus Christ. *Amen*

We bring before thee, O Lord, the troubles and perils of peoples and nations; the sighing of prisoners and captives; the sorrows of the bereaved; the necessities of strangers; the helplessness of the weak; the despondency of the weary; the failing powers of the aged. O Lord, draw near to each, for the sake of Jesus Christ our Lord. *Amen*

O loving Father, grant us to share in that gentleness of spirit which is a part of all true manliness, for the sake of Jesus Christ our Lord. *Amen*

O Lord Jesus Christ, who didst say to thy disciples, Come apart and rest awhile; grant us so to seek thee whom our souls desire to love, that we may both find and be found of thee. *Amen*

[11]

SIXTH DAY'S DEVOTION
Morning

11 O God, help us to be masters of ourselves that we may become the servants of others, and thus follow in the path of thy blessed Son, Jesus Christ our Lord. *Amen*

Read: *James 1 Not tempted of God*

We are not unmindful, O Lord, that we have stood so often where the crowd stood, abandoning thee. Forgive us, and grant that as we grow in age, we may grow in grace and in the knowledge of thee. *Amen*

Grant to us, O God, this day to do whatever duty lies before us with cheerfulness and sincerity of heart. Help us in all things fearlessly to do what we know is right. Remove from us all hypocrisy and pretense. Make us faithful, unselfish, and strong. And so bring us to the ending of the day unashamed and with a quiet mind, through Jesus Christ our Lord. *Amen*

We thank thee, O Lord our God, that thou art in every place; and that no space or distance can ever separate us from thee; that those who are absent from each other are still present with thee. Have in thy holy keeping those from whom we are now separated, and grant that both they and we, by drawing nearer unto thee, may be drawn nearer to one another in Jesus Christ our Lord. *Amen*

Blessed Lord, who wast tempted in all things like as we are, have mercy upon our frailty. Out of weakness give us strength. Support us in time of temptation. Embolden us in the time of danger. Help us to do thy work with good courage, and to continue thy faithful soldiers and servants unto our life's end, through Jesus Christ our Lord. *Amen*

SEVENTH DAY'S DEVOTION
Evening

---

14 Give us all courage, O Lord, to fight the battles we must fight, without and within; and the wisdom to hold sacred in all future days the visions and the hopes of suffering humanity. Grant us the realization that in times of trial we need not walk alone, for thou art our Father, and we the children of thy love. *Amen*

Read: *II Timothy 2:1-26   Endure hardness, a good soldier*

O God, from whom all holy desires, all good counsels, and all just works do proceed; give unto thy servants that peace which the world cannot give; that our hearts may be set to obey thy commandments; and also that by thee, we, being defended from the fear of our enemies, may pass our time in rest and quietness, through the merits of Jesus Christ, our Savior. *Amen*

Our Father, as we turn to the comfort of our rest, we remember those who must wake that we may sleep. Bless the guardians of peace who protect us against men of evil will, the watchers who save us from the terrors of fire, and all the many who carry on through the hours of the night the restless commerce of men on sea and land. We thank thee for their faithfulness and sense of duty. We pray for thy pardon if our covetousness or luxury makes their nightly toil more arduous. *Amen*

Be, Lord,
within me to strengthen me,
without me to preserve me,
over me to shelter me,
beneath me to support me,
before me to direct me,
behind me to bring me back,
round about me to fortify me.
In Christ. *Amen*

EIGHTH DAY'S DEVOTION
Morning

---

15 O God, the King eternal, who dividest the day from the darkness, and turnest the shadow of death into the morning: drive far off from us all wrong desires, incline our hearts to keep thy law, and guide our feet into the way of peace; that having done thy will with cheerfulness while it was day, we may, when night cometh, rejoice to give thee thanks, through Jesus Christ our Lord. *Amen*

Read: *Philippians 4:1-13 To be abased and to abound*

Almighty God, help us this day to arise out of the dreaminess of indolence, out of the gripping vice of low thoughts. Enable us by deliberate choice and resolute practice to set our minds upon those things which are true, honest, just, lovely, and of good report. Grant that day by day our minds may be so filled with great thoughts that our lives may steadily grow toward the measure of the stature of the fullness of Christ. *Amen*

Heavenly Father, let peace abound in our company. Purge out of every heart the lurking grudge. Give us grace and strength to forbear and persevere. Offenders ourselves, give us the grace to accept and forgive offenders. Forgetful, help us to bear cheerfully the forgetfulness of others. Give us courage and gaiety and the quiet mind, through Christ our Master. *Amen*

O God, who hast bound us together in this bundle of life, give us grace to understand how our lives depend upon the courage, the industry, the honesty, and the integrity of our fellow men; that we may be mindful of their needs, grateful for their faithfulness, and faithful in our responsibilities to them, through Jesus Christ our Lord. *Amen*

EIGHTH DAY'S DEVOTION
Evening

---

16 O God, save us from fever and restlessness, from haste and confusion, from noise and perpetual movement. Draw us back into those recesses of the Spirit where Jesus was one with thee. We praise thee that now, at this hour, we can be still and know that thou art God. *Amen*

Read: *Psalm 73   In the sanctuary I understood*

Father of our Lord, Jesus Christ, help me, I pray, to be a Christian in all the things I think and say and do, and in all the ways I go. Keep my heart restless until it finds its rest in thee. Save me from thinking that I am good, or that I can accomplish anything in my own strength. If I ever think that I am better than other people, stand quickly across my way and humble me. But raise me from the little deaths of my failures, for Jesus Christ's sake. Let me live entirely by the power that comes to me through him. Turn my thinking and talking and doing away from myself, and let me, giving myself up to thee, become a tool in thy hands for thine own purpose, and a true disciple of Jesus Christ, my Lord. *Amen*

Give me, O Lord, a steadfast heart, which no unworthy
　　thought can drag downward;
An unconquered heart, which no tribulation can wear
　　out;
An upright heart, which no unworthy purpose may tempt
　　aside.
Bestow upon me also, O Lord my God,
　　understanding to know thee,
　　diligence to seek thee,
　　wisdom to find thee,
　　and a faithfulness that may finally unite me with
　　thee;
Through Jesus Christ our Lord. *Amen*

Lord, I believe; help thou mine unbelief. *Amen*

NINTH DAY'S DEVOTION
Morning

17 O God, who hast folded back the black mantle of the night to clothe us in the golden glory of the day, chase from our hearts all gloomy thoughts and make us glad with the brightness of hope, that we may effectively aspire to unwon virtues, through Jesus Christ our Lord. *Amen*

Read: *Micah 6   God's requirements*

Thou hast showed us, O Lord, what is good; enable us, we beseech thee, to perform what thou dost require, even to do justly, to love mercy, and to walk humbly with our God. *Amen*

O God, the Lord of Life, we would dedicate ourselves this day:

Toward bringing justice into industry that everyone who works with hand or brain may share in the good life.

Toward opening closed doors of racial prejudice that every member of every race may share in all that frees a human spirit for abundant life.

Toward living so in personal relationships that everywhere we go there may be wings that try themselves in sunlight and find that life is good.

To join with other youth around the world to create lasting peace through means that we must find.

To strip from our religion all that is unreal and underneath the outer form to find a living God within a living universe, and to be ourselves more living in the living world of God.

To Him who waits to lead us into creative glorious adventuring, above all goals that we now see or even dream, we offer ourselves fully. *Amen*

O God, lead us, we beseech thee, to an ever deeper understanding of ourselves, and help us to be faithful interpreters of life to our fellow men. *Amen*

18 O God of peace, who hast taught us that in returning and rest we shall be saved, in quietness and confidence shall be our strength; by the might of thy Spirit lift us, we pray thee, to thy presence, where we may be still and know that thou art God, through Jesus Christ our Lord. *Amen*

Read: *Isaiah 55   Hear and live*

O divine Father, whose mercy ever awaits those who return unto thee in true lowliness and contrition of heart, hear now one humble servant who needs thy help. Bravely did I set out this morning upon the life of a new day; now I lie down ashamed and burdened with memories of things undone that ought to have been done and things done that ought not to have been done. Bring to me afresh, O God, thy healing and cleansing power, so that again I may lay hold of the salvation which thou hast offered me through Jesus Christ my Lord. *Amen*

O God, who speakest not in earthquake, wind, or fire, but ever through the still small voice in the soul of man, speak thou to us, and make us hear. Teach us to value a clear conscience, a quiet mind, a sense of fellowship with thee, before all the prizes and preferments the earth can bring. In the name of Christ we pray. *Amen*

O Lord, let me not henceforth desire health or life, except to spend them for thee, with thee, and in thee. Thou alone knowest what is good for me; do therefore what seemeth best to thee. Give to me, or take from me; conform my will to thine; and grant that with humble and perfect submission, and in holy confidence, I may receive the orders of thine eternal providence, and may equally adore all that comes to me from thee, through Jesus Christ our Lord. *Amen*

TENTH DAY'S DEVOTION
Morning

---

19 O God, before all voices which whisper to us of ease and caution and compromise, make us to feel the compulsion of thy desires, and the power of thy indwelling love, through Christ. *Amen*

Read: *Psalm 46 God our refuge and strength*

Creator Spirit, who broodest everlastingly over the lands and waters of earth, enduing them with forms and colors which no human skill can copy, give me today, I beseech thee, the mind and heart to rejoice in thy creation.

Forbid that I should walk through thy beautiful world with unseeing eyes:

Forbid that the lure of the marketplace should ever entirely steal my heart away from the love of the open acres and the green trees:

Forbid that under the low roof of workshop or office or study, I should ever forget thy great overarching sky:

Forbid that when all thy creatures are greeting the morning with songs and shouts of joy, I alone should wear a dull and sullen face:

Let the energy and vigor which in thy wisdom thou hast infused into every living thing stir today within my being, that I may not be among thy creatures as a sluggard and a drone:

And, above all, give me grace to use these beauties of earth around me and this eager stirring of life within me as a means whereby my soul may rise from creature to Creator, and from nature to nature's God. *Amen*

O Lord, suffer us not to turn in anger on him who has wronged us, seeking his hurt; lest we increase the sorrows of the world and taint our own souls with the poisoned sweetness of revenge. Make us determined to love even at cost to our pride, that so we may be bearers of thy peace on earth, through Christ. *Amen*

TENTH DAY'S DEVOTION
Evening

---

20 O thou who hast taught us that we are most truly free when we lose our wills in thine; help us to attain to this liberty by continued surrender unto thee, through Jesus Christ our Lord. *Amen*

Read: *Hebrews 12:1-11, 27-29   Run the race with patience*

Give us, O Lord, thy spirit of patience and perseverance for all who are stumbling and in danger of falling; and at all times when faith is difficult and opposition strong, grant us the help of thy grace to keep us from falling, and to present us at last without fault before thy throne, through Jesus Christ our Lord. *Amen*

O Jesus Christ, the Lord of all good life, who hast called us to help build the city of God; do thou enrich and purify our lives and deepen in us our discipleship. Help us daily to know more of thee, and through us, by the power of thy Spirit, show forth thyself to other men. Make us humble, brave, and loving; make us ready for adventure. We do not ask that thou wilt keep us safe, but that thou wilt keep us loyal; who for us didst face death unafraid, and dost live and reign with the Father and the Holy Spirit, God for ever and ever. *Amen*

Almighty God, if we have faltered because we are afraid, and if we are afraid because we dare not face the difficult tasks to which thou art calling us, grant us serene confidence and quiet courage and indomitable perseverance, that we may face discouragement, and failure, and even humiliating defeat in our endeavor to consecrate our bodies, minds, and souls for the advancement of thy kingdom. *Amen*

Let my prayer be set forth in thy sight as the incense; and let the lifting up of my hands be an evening sacrifice. *Amen*

[21]

ELEVENTH DAY'S DEVOTION
Morning

---

21 O Almighty God, from whom every good prayer cometh, and who pourest out on all who desire it the spirit of grace and supplication; deliver us when we draw nigh to thee from all coldness of heart and wanderings of mind, that with steadfast thoughts and kindled affections we may worship thee in spirit and in truth, through Jesus Christ our Lord. *Amen*

Read: *Revelation 3:14-22   Thou art neither cold nor hot*

O Lord Jesus Christ, who for our sake didst undergo want and shame and pain; we confess most humbly that we have refused to share the burden of thy cross, that we have denied thee rather than face mockery, and that we have put comfort and security before our duty. Forgive us our sins, help us to amend, and grant us the courage to endure, for thine own sake. *Amen*

O God, our Father, in the heaven above and in the earth beneath our feet, we find written large the evidences of some great plan we did not make. In the sweep of history, in the voices within our souls as we pause in quiet at the opening of a new day, we find also the witness of great purposes at work. In the teaching and life of great souls of many ages, and especially of Jesus Christ, we find the same thrust of ideals and commands that are more than earthly.
And so this morning we would seek the face of thine unseen self. We would know thy thoughts. We would be in harmony with thine eternal purposes. Give us a true conception of what our lives are for and what we may be, through Christ our Lord. *Amen*

Our Father, let me not only pray "Thy kingdom come," but do whatever one person can to let thy kingdom come through me. *Amen*

ELEVENTH DAY'S DEVOTION
Evening

---

22 O thou in whom we live and move and have our being: we offer and present unto thee ourselves, our souls and our bodies, our thoughts and our desires, our words and our deeds, to be a reasonable, holy, and living sacrifice unto thee, through Jesus Christ our Lord. *Amen*

Read: *Psalm 90 Thou hast been our dwelling place*

O God, thou eternal spirit indwelling the heart of man, take us at this hour away from things outward and visible, away from things of the moment. Make us conscious of things invisible and eternal. We thank thee that in Jesus Christ we can glimpse the world beyond the visible, and know the fullness of thy glory. May the mind and the life that was in him be also in us. Wilt thou guide, sustain, and keep us in all our ways, and through every day. Send us forward as willing instruments in thy hands, and grant us the assurance of thy sustaining presence. So in this world about us may we embody power, peace, and the strength which is of thee. *Amen*

O thou before whose eyes all human hearts lie bare and open, forbid that I should seek to hide from thee anything that I have this day done or thought or imagined. What must forever be hidden from the knowledge of others, that let me now openly acknowledge in thy presence. What no proper shame kept me from committing, that let no false shame keep me now from confessing. *Amen*

Abide with us, Lord, and with thy whole church. Abide with us in the end of the day, in the end of our life, in the end of the world. Abide with us with thy grace and bounty, with thy holy word and sacrament, with thy comfort and thy blessing. Abide with us and with all thy faithful. *Amen*

TWELFTH DAY'S DEVOTION
Morning

23 O God, save us this day from the distractions of vanity and the false lure of inordinate desires. In the press of life may we pass from duty to duty in tranquillity of heart and spread thy quietness to all who come near, through Christ. *Amen*

Read: *I John 4   Know ye the spirit of God*

God of each day, we bring to thee this day. It seems so slight a thing, and there seem to be so many like it, that we are tempted to hold it carelessly. We are thankful for its newness, its clean, untouched freshness, and for our chance to write upon its smooth, concise page. Forgive that we smear and blot it with our manifold mistakes. Stir our hearts and open our minds to its unique and varied possibilities, teach us discipline, guide us through each hour that we may use it to thy glory and to that of all men everywhere. *Amen*

Let us pray for Christians in temptation:
Those who receive the word with gladness, but in time of temptation fall away;
Those whose spiritual life is choked by materialism, by the cares and pleasures of this world;
Those whose faith is not strong enough to withstand the ridicule and antagonism of nonbelievers;
Those church members who do not persevere and who lapse into secularism;
Those who are tempted to fall back into their primitive religion of fear and the propitiation of angry deities;
Lord Jesus, we pray thee for our fellow Christians in all parts of the world and in this land who are facing difficulties, and who are tempted to turn back because the way is hard. Make them brave and steadfast, and may their loyal witness draw others to thee, for thine own name's sake. *Amen*

TWELFTH DAY'S DEVOTION
Evening

---

24 O Master, as this day closes and passes from our control, the sense of our shortcomings is quick within us, and we seek thy pardon. Defend us from all fretfulness, and suffer us not to cherish dark thoughts of resentment or revenge. So fill us with thy abounding love and peace that no ill-will may be left in our hearts as we turn to our rest: through Jesus Christ. *Amen*

Read: *Luke 6:20-38 Forgive, and be forgiven*

Almighty God, whose dwelling is with the humble and contrite heart, grant us thy mercy. For all that has been evil in our lives, for unholy thought and impure motives, for scorn of goodness, trifling with truth, and indifference to beauty, for all our wanderings from the better way, forgive us, O Lord. For all the wrong we have done our fellow men, for unkind words and untruthful speech, for loss of temper and irritating conduct, for neglect of charity and failure in justice, for arrogant pride and contempt of the lowly, forgetfulness of others' pain, and advantage taken of others' weakness; for whatever one may rightfully hold against us, forgive us, O Lord. Give us grace to follow the Master steadfastly. *Amen*

O Master, thou hast taught us that our sins may be forgiven only as we forgive others; and that the gifts we bring to thine altar can be offered in true communion with thee only after we have set our souls at peace with our brothers; now, grant that we may freely forgive any against whom we have borne resentment or ill-feeling. Heal them from the arrows of our sharp thoughts, and open our eyes that we may see in them the beauty of thy Spirit. Fill our hearts with the grace of thy love toward all persons, especially toward any from whom we have been estranged. So may we be clear channels for thy Spirit, sensitive to thy leading, and free to follow thy will. *Amen*

[25]

THIRTEENTH DAY'S DEVOTION
Morning

25 O God, may there be nothing in this day's work of which we shall be ashamed when the sun has set, nor in the eventide of our life when our task is done and we go to our eternal home to meet thy face. *Amen*

Read: *Psalm 121   I will lift up my eyes unto the hills*

Blessed art thou, O Lord, our God, the God of our fathers, who turnest the shadow of death into the morning; and lightenest the face of the earth; who separatest darkness from the face of the light; and banishest night and bringest back the day; who lightenest mine eyes, that I sleep not in death; who deliverest me from the terror by night, from the pestilence that walketh in darkness; who drivest sleep from mine eyes, and slumber from mine eyelids; who makest the outgoings of the morning and evening to praise thee; because I laid me down and slept and rose up again, for the Lord sustained me; because I waked and beheld; and my sleep was sweet unto me. *Amen*

O God, our Father, who hast taught us to see thy work not alone in the strange and wonderful, but also in the common things of life, in the great laws of the universe, and in the mind and spirit of men, help us to understand that in our own souls thy voice speaks clearly. Teach us to heed that voice, and to work out as Jesus did thine own high purpose for each one of us. *Amen*

O God, the Creator of all things, who art perpetually renewing the face of the world and hast created us anew in Christ Jesus, grant that in the worship of thee and in communion with thee thy creative energy may more and more flood our lives, so that we may play our part in the fulfillment of thy purpose, which transcends all that we can think or understand. *Amen*

THIRTEENTH DAY'S DEVOTION
Evening

---

26 O God, forgive us when in our pride and conceit we think that but for us thy purposes would fail. We are grateful that thou dost make us to know that while we sleep, the stars yet travel in their courses, and the grasses of the field grow, and that even should our hands suddenly fall lifeless before an unfinished task, still thy work presses on. *Amen*

Read: *Ecclesiastes 12   Man goes to his enduring home*

Almighty God, lift us out of our shadows into thy light; out of our fears into thy fortifying thoughts; out of our perplexities into thy clear truth; out of our burdens into thy strength; out of our foolish and disappointed purposes into thy holy and blessed will; out of our troubles into thy peace. Give us that great faith in thee which will fill us with peace from the known that surrounds us, and from the unknown that is above and beyond us, through Jesus Christ our Lord. *Amen*

O God our Father, forgive us our preoccupation with trivial things in days of solemn import for the future. Forgive us the personal selfishness that blinds our eyes to the needs of our fellows, that stops our ears from hearing the cries of the wounded, that steels our hearts so that we do not really feel the wordless despair of thousands for whom all but life itself is gone. Through Christ. *Amen*

Give us, O Lord, such a realization of our sonship to thee, that we may look upon this wonderful world, its beauty and its treasures, as thy gift, and so recognize always that all we have must be used in accordance with thy will. *Amen*

FOURTEENTH DAY'S DEVOTION
Morning

27 Almighty God, we thank thee for rest and health; for work to do, and strength to do it; and for all the surroundings of our life that make it desirable and enjoyable. Do thou raise our thoughts and purify our aspirations. Strengthen our wills, we beseech thee, on the side of what is right and good, and against what is wrong and evil, through Jesus Christ our Lord. *Amen*

Read: *Amos 5   Seek good, and not evil*

Our Father, lead us this day to meet some brother in his need, to go the second mile in carrying the cross of someone else. Enlarge our horizons so that every barrier of class and nation and race shall be put aside before the claims of our brotherhood in Christ. *Amen*

Give us clean hands, clean words, and clean thoughts. Help us to stand for the hard right against the easy wrong. Save us from habits that harm. Teach us to work as hard and play as fair in thy sight alone as if all the world saw. Forgive us when we are unkind, and help us to forgive those who are unkind to us. Keep us ready to help others at some cost to ourselves. Send us chances to do a little good every day, and so to grow more like Christ. *Amen*

O God our Father, touch our hearts with a deep yet humble sense of our kinship with thee, for we are thy children. Remind us anew that every hour of this day is thy priceless gift of time and life for each of us to use; and that these hours are gifts which pass and do not come again. Grant that when this day is over, and darkness falls upon the earth, we shall not have lived a single hour in vain. We ask it in the name of him whose hours on earth were few, yet whose life none of us can ever wholly forget. *Amen*

FOURTEENTH DAY'S DEVOTION
Evening

---

28 Be present, O merciful God, and protect us through the silent hours of this night, so that we who are wearied by the changes and chances of this fleeting world may repose upon thine unchanging love, through Jesus Christ our Lord. *Amen*

Read: *Psalm 16   I will bless the Lord*

O God of the prophets, the saints and seers of every age, God of the humble, God of the contrite heart, speak to us at this hour. Help us to hear this night the music of the stars, the song of life, the call of mankind to every valiant heart. Redeem this day for us; lift us out of its ruts of selfishness and indifference, its self-satisfaction and laziness. Make us glad that our lives are matched against human need, and that we can answer, in the name of Jesus Christ. *Amen*

Lord of the evening hour, who hast often met with us at the close of day, be our refuge now from the noise of the world and the care of our own spirits. Grant us thy peace. Let not the darkness of our ignorance and folly, of our sorrow and sin, hide thee from from us. Through Christ our Lord. *Amen*

O Divine Love who dost everlastingly stand outside the closed doors of the souls of men, knocking ever and again, wilt thou not now give me grace to throw open all my soul's doors? Tonight let every bolt and bar be drawn that has hitherto robbed my life of air and light and love. *Amen*

Make us of quick and tender conscience, O Lord, that understanding we may obey every word of thine, and discerning may follow every suggestion of thine indwelling Spirit. Speak, Lord, for thy servant heareth. *Amen*

PART II. BIBLE STUDY IN WORSHIP

Bible Study in Worship

[A new eagerness to know what the Bible really says has led an increasing number of young people to approach it seriously, often with prayer. The themes dealt with here can only point to the vast riches of the Bible, but they may lead to further exploration. Pertinent passages, verses, and prayers may well be added to the outline.

Each numbered section (after the first) should take twenty to thirty minutes. All may be used either for individual worship or for groups. A leader may read the prayers, the others the Scripture, or vice versa; or members of a circle may take successive turns. It may be helpful to use No. 29 as a preface to each period of worship. In any case, the first person to speak should say "Let us pray" or otherwise mark the attitude of prayer.]

29 PRAYERS ON APPROACHING THE BIBLE

O God, open up unto us thy Word, that it may not remain to us unknown, formidable, a book which fails to touch our lives. Guide us to know thee and reveal thyself by thy Word. Set forth thy truth through those who know its power and its eternal applications. Too often we find Scripture baffling and remote from our interests. Help us at such times, O God, to study it aright, that it may open up to us the treasures of human and divinely inspired experience within it. May it become to us a book of life, speaking across the centuries to us who face the needs and problems of this day. In the name of our Lord and Maker we pray. *Amen*

O God, grant that thy Word may be a lamp unto our feet, and a light unto our path. Give us wisdom to discern its teaching and patience to apply it, with such sincerity of heart that our deeds may conform to its instruction, through Jesus Christ, our Master and our Lord. *Amen*

Blessed Lord, who hast caused all Holy Scriptures to be written for our learning: grant that we may in such wise hear them, read, mark, learn, and inwardly digest them that by patience, and comfort of thy Holy Word, we may embrace and ever hold fast the blessed hope of everlasting life, which thou hast given us in our Savior, Jesus Christ. *Amen*

Almighty and most merciful God, who hast given the Bible to be the revelation of thy great love to man, and of thy power and will to save him; grant that our study of it may not be made in vain by the callousness or carelessness of our hearts; but that by it we may be confirmed in penitence, lifted to hope, made strong for service, and filled with the true knowledge of thee and of thy Son Jesus Christ. *Amen*

O Lord, let not thy Word become a judgment upon us, that we hear it and do it not, that we know it and love it not, that we believe it and obey it not. We pray in Christ. *Amen*

Theme One: Know That I Am God

30 GOD'S WORK AND HIS GLORY
O Hidden Source of life, let me now meditate upon the great and gracious plan by which thou hast brought it to pass that a mortal man like me should look up to thee and call thee Father.

In the beginning thou, the Uncreated, putting forth thy
    creative power:
And then space and time and material substance:
The atom and the molecule and crystalline forms:
And then the first germ of life:
And then the long upward striving of life:
All things that creep and fly, the beasts of the forest, the
    fowls of the air, the fish of the sea:

And then the gradual dawn of intelligence:
And at last the making of man:
And the beginning of history:
And the first altar, and the first prayer.

Let me keep in mind how thy whole creation groans and travails, waiting for the perfect appearing of the sons of God; and let me welcome every influence of thy Spirit upon my own that may the more speedily make for that end. In Christ. *Amen*

Read: *Genesis 1:1-5   In the beginning*

I have thought upon thee, O Lord,
when I was waking,
for thou hast been my helper.
Blessed art thou, O Lord,
who madest the two lights, sun and moon,
greater and lesser,
and the stars
for light, for signs, for seasons;
spring, summer, autumn, winter,
days, weeks, months, years,
to rule over day and night.

Read: *Psalm 8   How excellent thy name*

Eternal Father, in a generation among whom thou hast opened up vast new marvels of thy universe, quicken our faith to match our knowledge. As of old, may the timeless patterns of day and night lead us to ponder thy law written into all reality, thy truth spoken most clearly to our hearts in Christ. *Amen*

Read: *Psalm 19   The heavens declare*

Most high, most great and good Lord, to thee belong praises, glory, and every blessing!

Blessed be thou, my Lord, for the gift of all thy creatures; and especially for our brother the sun, by whom the day is enlightened. He is radiant and bright, and of great splendor, bearing witness to thee, O my God.

Blessed be thou, my Lord, for our sister the moon,

and for the stars; thou hast formed them in the heavens, fair and clear.

Blessed be thou, my Lord, for our brother the wind, for the air, for cloud, and calm, for every kind of weather, for by them thou dost sustain all creatures.

Blessed be thou, my Lord, for our sister water, which is very useful, humble, chaste, and precious.

Blessed be thou, my Lord, for our brother fire, gay, noble, and beautiful, untamable and strong; by whom thou dost illume the night.

Blessed be thou, my Lord, for our mother the earth, who sustains and nourishes us, who brings forth all kinds of fruit, herbs, and bright-hued flowers.

Blessed be thou, my Lord, for those who pardon for love of thee, who patiently bear infirmity and tribulation. Happy are those who abide in peace, for by thee, Most High, they will be crowned.

Blessed be thou, my Lord, for our sister death of the body, from whom no living man can escape. Happy are they who at the hour of death are found in obedience to thy holy will.

Praise ye, and bless ye my Lord! Give him thanks, and serve him with great humility! *Amen*

Read: *Job 38:1-36 Who teaches the Almighty?*

O thou, who art an unknown God to millions of men in our time, grant us boldness and skill to declare thee openly among both the wise and the unlearned; that a redeeming awareness of thy work and thy glory may swiftly increase through all the earth, in Christ. *Amen*

Read: *Acts 17:22-34 "Ye men of Athens"*

31 GOD'S JUSTICE (OLD TESTAMENT)
Almighty God, grant us to know anew in this day what is right and wrong. We live among a people careless of thy law; we find within our own selves confusion and rebellion. O thou in whose eternal judgment all na-

[36]

tions rise and fall, all men and their pretensions are weighed, show us thy right for our time. So may we live by thy law, and Christ being our redeemer, fulfill thy commandment to be perfect through him. *Amen*

Read: *Exodus 20:1-17   The ten commandments*

Almighty God, show us thy mercy; that we who put no trust in our own merits may not be dealt with after the severity of thy judgment, but according to thy mercy, through Jesus Christ our Lord. *Amen*

Read: *Ezekiel 18:20-28   Individual responsibility*

We cry to thee for justice, O Lord, for our soul is weary with the iniquity of greed. Behold the servants of mammon, who defy thee and drain their fellow men for gain; who grind down the strength of the workers by merciless toil and fling them aside when they are mangled and worn; who rackrent the poor and make dear the space and air which thou hast made free; who paralyze the hand of justice by corruption and blind the eyes of the people by lies; who have brought upon thy Church the contempt of men and have cloaked their extortion with the gospel of thy Christ. Shake their souls with awe of thee that they may cease. Help us with clean hands to tear the web which they have woven about us and to turn our people back to thy law. In Christ. *Amen*

Read: *Amos 4:6-13; 8:4-10   Prepare to meet God*

Read: *Micah 6:1-8   What doth the Lord require?*

Write upon our hearts, O Lord God, the lessons of thy holy Word, and grant that we may all be doers of the same, and not forgetful hearers only; through Jesus Christ our Lord. *Amen*

32 GOD'S JUSTICE (NEW TESTAMENT)
Let us humbly acknowledge before God that we have not kept his Law. We have not fulfilled the purpose of our Creator, but have sought to take control of

our own destiny; we have devastated the earth, and exploited the lower creation. We have lived in fear, and fear has made us cruel. We have sought to be as God, and have fallen lower than the beasts.

But as his majesty is, so is his mercy.

Thank God that in Christ there is a new creation, and that in Christ all things return to him in whom they had their origin. Thank God that although he does not explain, he does redeem.

Read: *Matthew 5:17-20   To fulfill, not destroy*

Read: *Matthew 21:33-46   The vineyardmen*

Lord, thou hast shown us according to thy holy Word, that they who come to thee shall in no wise be cast out, while those who refuse thy love shall not behold thy face. Grant, we pray thee, that having ever in remembrance our frail condition and our wayward wills, we may use our freedom not to our own condemnation but to thy honor and glory, through Jesus Christ our Lord.

V. From the despising of thy mercy and the spurning of thy love;
R. *Good Lord, deliver us.*
V. From pride in our sufficiency and contentment with our ignorance;
R. *Good Lord, deliver us.*
V. From a rebellious will and all hardening of heart;
R. *Good Lord, deliver us.*
V. From the refusal of charity and the loneliness of the damned;
R. *Good Lord, deliver us.*
V. From the darkness of our self-destruction, and the pains of thy absence;
R. *Good Lord, deliver us.*
V. From hell and from damnation;
R. *Good Lord, deliver us. Amen*

Read: *Matthew 25:31-46   Sheep divided from goats*

Almighty and everlasting God, who art always **more** ready to hear than we to pray, and art wont to give **more** than either we desire, or deserve: pour down upon us the abundance of thy mercy; forgiving us those things whereof our conscience is afraid, and giving us those good things which we are not worthy to ask, but through the merits and mediation of Jesus Christ, thy Son, our Lord. *Amen*

Read: *Acts 3:13-26   Turn from iniquity, find God*

33 GOD'S BOUNDLESS LOVE

O God, who hast prepared for those who love thee such good things as pass man's understanding; pour into our hearts such love toward thee, that we, loving thee above all things, may obtain thy promises, which exceed all that we can desire, through Jesus Christ our Lord. *Amen*

Read: *Psalm 23   The Lord is my shepherd*

Our heavenly Father, who by thy love hast made us, and through thy love hast kept us, and in thy love wouldst make us perfect, we humbly confess that we have not loved thee with all our heart and soul and mind and strength, and that we have not loved one another as Christ hath loved us. Thy life is within our souls, but our selfishness hath hindered thee. We have resisted thy Spirit. We have neglected thine inspirations.

Forgive what we have been; help us to amend what we are; and in thy Spirit direct what we shall be; that thou mayest come into the full glory of thy creation, in us and in all men, through Jesus Christ our Lord. *Amen*

Read: *Luke 6:27-38   Love is of God*

O God of mercy, who so carest for me as if thou hadst none else to care for, yet carest for all even as thou carest for me; I commend to thee my own needs but also the needs of all this world of men to which I belong. *Amen*

Read: *Luke 15:3-32   Reclaiming the lost*

[39]

O Lord of life and Lord of love, love us into life, and give us life to love thee. Grant us life enough to put life into all things. Touch those of us whose life is more barren than it need be—lacking knowledge and beauty, filled with petty interests and foolish cares. Forgive us that our life is so poor. Grant that in us, short-lived, vexed with cares, hungry, thirsty, dying as we are, thy Spirit may so come and dwell, that the beauty of the Lord may be upon us, and the work of our hands be established: through Christ our Lord. *Amen*

Read: *Romans 5:1-11   God commendeth his love*

O God, mercifully grant unto us that the fire of thy love may burn up in us all things that displease thee, and make us meet for thy heavenly kingdom. *Amen*

Read: *I John 3:1-2   What manner of love*

34 **GOD'S ABIDING PRESENCE**
Fix thou our steps, O Lord, that we stagger not at the uneven motions of the world, but go steadily on our way; neither accommodating our journey to the weather we meet, nor turning aside for anything that befalls us. *Amen*

Read: *Psalm 91   In the secret place*

Grant unto us, Almighty God, thy peace that passeth understanding; that we, amid the storms and troubles of this our life, may rest in thee, knowing that all things are in thee, under thy care, governed by thy will, guarded by thy love. So with a quiet heart may we see the storms of life, the cloud, and the thick darkness; ever rejoicing to know that the darkness and the light are both alike to thee. Guide, guard, and govern us even to the end, that none of us may fail to lay hold upon the immortal life. *Amen*

Read: *Psalm 139:1-12, 17-18, 23-24   Searched and known*

O God, thou hast made us for thyself, and our hearts are restless until they find their rest in thee. We give thee thanks for this divine indwelling unrest; help us so to trust its leadings that we fail not of the things which belong unto our peace. *Amen*

Read: *Isaiah 40:28-31 On wings as eagles*

O God, who understandest the secret longings of our hearts, and who hast reserved some portion of thy healing grace for the particular need of each one of us; we seek in thee that peace and purpose which the world can neither give nor take away:

To each of us drifting comfortably, yet unawakened, grant now a baptism into a realization of the world's need;

To each of us plagued with a divided self, with conflicting hopes, with uncertainty of the future, and with bitter disappointment in the present; grant, Lord, Christ's unity of purpose, his clear vision, his welcome to life and death, and his triumph over defeat.

To each of us who hates another, or does not care that others' lives are unfulfilled through our selfishness, give a contrite heart, a mellowed spirit, some touch of the love of God that forgives.

Lord God, let no sophistication, coldness, or bleak theorizing keep us from that humility and simplicity which may send us back to see the glory of the commonplace: in the name of him who unveils the secret of life, our Lord and Master Jesus Christ. *Amen*

Read: *John 14:15-21 I am with you always*

O thou who wast, and art, and art to come, I thank thee that this Christian way whereon I walk is no untried or uncharted road, but a road beaten hard by the footsteps of saints, apostles, prophets, and martyrs. I thank thee for the fingerposts and danger signals with which it is marked at every turning and which may be known to me through the study of the Bible, and of all history, and of all the great literature of the world. Beyond all, I give thee devout and humble thanks for the great gift of Jesus Christ, the Pioneer of our faith. I praise thee that thou hast caused me to be born in an age and in a land which has known his name, and that I am not called upon to face any temptation or trial which he did not first endure. Forbid it, holy Lord, that I should fail to profit by these great memories of the ages that are gone by, or to enter into the glorious inheritance which thou hast prepared for me: through Jesus Christ my Lord. *Amen*

Read: *Psalm 118:1-9   Better to trust in God*

Theme Two: He Sent His Son Our Lord

35 THE INCARNATION

Blessed be God for his incarnation.

Thou little Son of God, laid in a manger, we adore thee for thy coming! Now God is of our image, God is of our flesh and blood! Now there is no difference at all between thy flesh and ours! Thou art our savior and our brother who liest in a crib! Thou liest in our misery, sharest our needs, assurest us of our glory. Alleluia! *Amen*

Read: *John 1:1-14   Word made flesh*

Reveal thyself to us, O God, as thou didst to all the world in Christ our Lord, who for us men and our salvation came down from heaven; that drawn by the star of his appearing, we may lay the treasures of our life at his feet; whom, with thee and the Holy Spirit, we worship and glorify as one God. *Amen*

Read: *Matthew 2:1-12   Visit of the magi*

O sing unto the Lord a new song: sing unto the Lord, all the earth! Arise, shine; for thy light is come!

O Lord our God, if this day we cannot sing to thee a new song, touch the old song of the saints with a new

[42]

power for us, and make us also children of the light, through Jesus Christ our Lord. *Amen*

Read: *Luke 2:8-20   Vision of the shepherds*

O Father, who long ago didst send thy singing angels through the midnight of the sleeping world, to tell the shepherds Christ was born in Bethlehem; awaken our drowsy hearts to that same message of redeeming love, and stir our darkness that we may hear again love's wonder song. And as they sped to carry the glad tidings and to adore the newborn King, help us also to proclaim thy goodness as heralds of thy pardon to all who are in sin, and of thy mercy to all who are in pain, sin's bitter shadow: through Christ our Lord.

O Lord, the angels' song has been silenced by the clang of the daily conflict; the feet of the toiling generations have well-nigh obliterated the way of the pilgrims to Bethlehem. But we give thee thanks, O Lord, that yet there are hours of quiet when the stillness of starry places steals over life's din again; that yet there are souls that hear, and longing spirits that listen, and pure in heart who can see the marks of thy coming, to heal and help and bless poor stricken humanity. We bless thy love, O Lord. *Amen*

Master and Lord,
We bless thee that thou, who art omnipotent,
Dost strip thyself of omnipotence to put on our human
    flesh:
That thou, who art all purity and love
Dost graciously enter these strained and selfish hearts of
    ours.
We bless thee that thou dwellest not afar in heaven,
Beyond and above thy tortured world,
Serene and carefree in thy cool paradise;
But that thou art here amongst us in the sultry darkness.
We thank thee that thou hast overcome the world in
    Christ. *Amen*

Read: *II Corinthians 5:17-20   God was in Christ*

[43]

O Lord God, let me not rest content with such an ideal of manhood as men have known apart from Christ. Rather let such a mind be in me as was in him. Let me not rest till I come to the stature of his own fullness. Let me listen to Christ's question: What do ye more than others? And so may the threefold Christian graces of faith, hope, and love be more and more formed within me, until all my walk and conversation be such as becometh the gospel of Christ. *Amen*

Read: *Philippians 2:5-11   He humbled himself*

O Lord Jesus Christ, who art the truth incarnate and the teacher of the faithful; let thy spirit overshadow us in reading thy Word, and conform our thoughts to thy revelation; that learning of thee with honest hearts, we may be rooted and built up in thee; who livest and reignest with the Father and the Holy Spirit, one God, world without end. *Amen*

Read: *Hebrews 1:1-4   Spoken unto us by his Son*

36 JESUS' MINISTRY
Read: *Mark 1:1-11   His baptism*

Almighty God, whose blessed Son shared his people's renewal of righteousness in baptism, and who heard therein thy summons to his kingly mission; grant us in his name both cleansing and commitment to thy will for all men. *Amen*

Read: *Luke 4:16-21   The Spirit is upon me*

O Lord, move us by thine example to show kindness and do good. Grant us such patience and forbearance with all sufferers, gracious or ungracious, grateful or ungrateful, that in our stumbling walk and scant measure they may yet discern a vestige of thee and give thee the glory. *Amen*

Read: *Mark 1:32-45   Healing, preaching, praying*

Set before our minds, O heavenly Father, the example of our Lord Jesus Christ, who when he was upon earth found joy in doing the will of him that sent him, and in finishing his work. When many are coming and going, and there is little quiet, give us grace to remember him who knew neither impatience of spirit nor confusion of work, but in the midst of all his labors kept a tranquil heart, at leisure from itself to serve and sympathize. Through Christ. *Amen*

Read: *John 3:1-8   Ye must be born again*

Grant, we beseech thee, Almighty God, that the new birth of thine only-begotten Son in the flesh may set us free, who are held under the yoke of sin; through the same Jesus Christ. *Amen*

Read: *Luke 9:1-6, 18-36   The transfiguration and the disciples*

O God, too often we take thee for granted, offer thee dull phrase and empty gesture for worship, and fail to recognize thy likeness among our fellow men. Surround us with the bright cloud of thy glory, that we may see thee as thou art, and know thee as the Son of Man in our midst: for his sake. *Amen*

Read: *Luke 19:33-40   The way of palms*

Keep us at thy side, O God, not only when the world hails thee king, but when all men desert thee and scorn thy cross. As we are the companions of thy triumph, make us sharers also of thy suffering for mankind; to the end that both cross and crown may be marks of the redemption thou hast given us in Christ Jesus. *Amen*

Read: *Mark 14:16-24   The Lord's Supper*

O Son of Man, we praise thee for those whom thou didst gather at thy table:

For the impulsive, inspired to declare great things of thee, yet ready instantly to forsake thee:
   these ways we know in our own heart.

[45]

For the half-doubtful, never fully comprehending, seeking added proof of thy high claim, even while continuing to follow thee:
these ways we know in our own heart.
For the traitorous, disappointed at the cost of discipleship and resenting thy quiet ministry of love, betraying thee even while being called thy friend:
these ways we know in our own heart.
For the drowsy, eager to watch and pray with thee, but not strong enough to stay awake and share thine anguish:
these ways we know in our own heart.
For the mildly effective, wondering why their power to heal was far less than their Master's, because they had not prayed enough:
these ways we know in our own heart.
For the distracted, wistful to stay and carry out old duties before fully following thee:
these ways we know in our own heart.
For the small-visioned, speaking and healing in Christ's name but discontent that others not of their company found power also in him:
these ways we know in our own heart.
For the impatient, wishing to call down fire from heaven to accomplish what thou wouldst do by the slow winning witness of love:
these ways we know in our own heart.

O thou who knewest what was in man, and didst share every common meal with those whose ways we know in our own heart, be ever host at our board, ever the breaker of bread, ever blessing, ever blessed among us! *Amen*

37 JESUS' SUFFERING AND DEATH
May this mind be in us that was in Christ Jesus.

Let us remember Jesus:
Who, though he was rich, yet for our sakes became poor and dwelt among us.

Who was content to be subject to his parents, the child of a poor man's home.

Who lived for nearly thirty years the common life, earning his living with his own hands and declining no humble tasks.

Whom the common people heard gladly, for he understood their ways.

Let us remember Jesus:

Who was mighty in deed, healing the sick and the disordered, using for others the powers he would not invoke for himself.

Who refused to force men's allegiance.

Who was Master and Lord to his disciples, yet who was among them as their companion and as one who served.

Whose meat was to do the will of the Father who sent him.

Let us remember Jesus:

Who loved men, yet retired from them to pray; who rose a great while before day, watched through a night, stayed in the wilderness, went up into a mountain, sought a garden.

Who prayed for the forgiveness of those who rejected him, and for the perfecting of those who received him.

Who observed good customs, but defied conventions which did not serve the purposes of God.

Who hated sin because he knew the cost of pride and selfishness, of cruelty and impurity, to man, and still more to his Father in heaven.

Let us remember Jesus:

Who believed in men to the last and never despaired of them.

Who through all disappointment never lost heart.

Who disregarded his own comfort and convenience and thought first of other's needs, and though he suffered long, was always kind.

Who, when he was reviled, reviled not again, and when he suffered, threatened not.

Who humbled himself and carried obedience to the

point of death, even death on the cross, and endured faithful to the end.

O Christ, our only Savior, so come to dwell in us that we may go forth with the light of thy hope in our eyes, and with thy faith and love in our hearts. *Amen*

Read: *Isaiah 53:1-6   Despised and rejected*

Almighty God, who hast shown us in the life and teaching of thy Son the true way of blessedness: thou hast also shown us in his suffering and death that the path of love may lead to the cross, and the reward of faithfulness may be a crown of thorns. Give us grace to learn these hard lessons. May we have such fellowship with him in his sorrow, that we may know the secret of his strength and peace, and see even in our darkest hour of trial and anguish the shining of the eternal light. *Amen*

Read: *Mark 14:29-42   Gethsemane*

Deliver us, O God, from complacency in judging evil in our fellows, knowing that thou alone canst truly weigh any man's merit. As we behold betrayal and perfidy in others, may our indignation point us inward to the disloyalty and dishonor to thy gospel which lurk within us, that in humility and contrition we may be freed from our sin by penitence and forgiveness in Christ. *Amen*

Read: *Mark 14:43-50   Betrayal by Judas*

We glorify and praise
Him whom Judas sold; *O Lord, forgive those faithless through love of riches and the world's deceits.*
Him whom Peter denied; *Our Father, forgive the timorous and those betrayed by sudden fear.*
Him whom Caiaphas condemned; *O God, forgive those who have seen and hated both Christ and thee.*
Him whom Pilate sentenced; *forgive, O Lord, those who bow before the judgment of men.*
Him whom the soldiers crucified and the crowd blasphemed; *forgive, Our Father, the ignorant who know not what they do.*

[48]

Him to whom the dying thief appealed; *forgive, O God, the penitent and accept the dying. Amen*

Read: *Mark 14:53-65   The trial*

O Lord Jesus Christ, who for our sakes didst undergo want and shame and pain, we confess most humbly that we have refused to share the burden of thy cross; that we have denied thee rather than face mockery, and have sought comfort and security. Forgive our sin, help us to amend, and give us courage to endure. *Amen*

Read: *Mark 14:66-72   Peter's denial*

Grant, O most gracious God, that we may carry with us the remembrance of the sufferings and death of Jesus Christ our Lord.

For the power of his cross in the history of the world since he came:
For all who have taken up their own crosses and have followed him:
For the noble army of martyrs and for all who are willing to die that others may live:
For all suffering freely chosen for noble ends, for pain bravely endured, for temporal sorrows that have been used for the building up of eternal joys:

We praise and bless thy holy name. *Amen*

Read: *Mark 15:15-38   The crucifixion*

38 JESUS' TRIUMPH

Thou brightness of God's glory and express image of his Person, whom death could not conquer nor the tomb imprison; as thou hast shared our mortal frailty in the flesh, help us to share thine immortal triumph in the spirit. Let no shadow of the grave affright us and no fear of darkness turn our hearts from thee. Reveal thyself to us as the first and the last, the Living One, our immortal Savior and Lord. *Amen*

Read: *I Corinthians 15:1-26   Paul on the resurrection*

[49]

O God, who for our redemption didst give thine only-begotten Son to the death of the cross, and by his glorious resurrection hast delivered us from the power of our enemy; grant us so to die daily unto sin, that we may evermore live with him in the joy of his resurrection: through the same Jesus Christ our Lord. *Amen*

Read: *Luke 24:1-12 Easter morning*

O blessed Christ, who didst draw near to thy disciples as they walked together by the way and were sad, so draw near to us as we journey along our daily way. Open to us the meaning of life, and reveal thyself as our strength and our companion, as thou art our Lord and Savior evermore. *Amen*

Read: *Luke 24:13-35 The talk with two*

O God, who through the resurrection of thy Son didst bestow life and freedom upon the world, continue, we beseech thee, these thy gifts unto thy people, that we may both walk in perfect freedom and attain unto life eternal: through the same Jesus Christ our Lord. *Amen*

Read: *Luke 24:36-40 Appearance to many*

O God, who knowest thy earthly family as neither Jew nor Greek, male nor female, bond nor free, but as children standing in equal need and all sharing thy fatherly love; grant that thy Church, being quickened by thy love, may manifest to the world the unity to which thou hast called it. By the gospel of thy Son and the fellowship of his disciples, bring healing to the world. *Amen*

Read: *Matthew 28:16-20 Go into all the world*

39 JESUS' EXAMPLE AND TEACHING

Bless me, O God, with love of thee and of my neighbor. Give me peace of conscience, the command of my affections; and for the rest, thy will be done. O King of peace, keep us in love and charity. *Amen*

Read: *Mark 12:28-31 The two commandments*

O Lord, hear our prayer:

That no more may the Lord Christ be crowded from our
     lives, but that he may come and dwell in our hearts;
That as we respect and reverence Christ's character, we
     may seek ourselves to imitate it;
That we who attempt to follow Christ may use and not
     neglect or despise his appointed means of prayer
     and sacrament.

Jesus said "Why sleep ye? Rise and pray."

O thou who didst give such grace to the first followers
     of thy Son, that they readily obeyed his calling and
     followed him without delay, quicken us in our dis-
     cipline before him this day. *Amen*

Read: *Matthew 5:13-16   Ye are the salt*

Holy God, to whose service I long ago dedicated my soul
and life, I grieve and lament before thee that I am still
so prone to sin and so little inclined to obedience:

     So much attached to the pleasure of sense, so negli-
     gent of things spiritual:
     So prompt to gratify my body, so slow to nourish
     my soul:
     So greedy for present delight, so indifferent to last-
     ing blessedness:
     So fond of idleness, so indisposed for labor:
     So soon at play, so late at prayer:
     So brisk in the service of self, so slack in the service
     of others:
     So eager to get, so reluctant to give:
     So lofty in my profession, so low in my practice:
     So full of good intentions, so backward to fulfill
     them:
     So severe with my neighbors, so indulgent with
     myself:
     So eager to find fault, so resentful at being found
     fault with:
     So little able for great tasks, so discontented with
     small ones:

[51]

So weak in adversity, so swollen and self-satisfied in
prosperity:
So helpless apart from thee, and yet so little willing
to be bound to thee.

O merciful heart of God, grant me yet forgiveness, for
his holy name's sake. *Amen*

Read: *Matthew 5:27-32   The motive is deeper*

O Christ, at whose word the wind and waves were still,
rebuke we pray thee the violence of men, and usher in
the day of brotherhood, that we may truly serve thee.

Lord of life, master of men, pattern of gentleness,
    Hear us, Lord Jesus.
By the prophets' dream of old,
    Grant us victory over war.
By the angels' song of peace,
    Raise up leaders of goodwill.
By thy gospel's words of love,
    Help us to love our enemies.
By thy sacrificial death,
    Teach the nations self-denial.
By the kingdom thou hast promised,
    Come to rule the hearts of men.
By the kingdom thou hast promised,
    Make the nations one in Christ. Amen

Read: *Matthew 5:39-48   Love your enemies*

God of our prayers, dwelling in eternity and yet closer
than breathing, nearer than hands and feet, redeem the
shallow and smooth words with which often we seek thy
presence. Deliver us from devotions voiced for others'
hearing rather than for thee, from words spoken by our
lips rather than in our minds. As thy Son our Lord
taught his disciples to pray in words which should witness that they had been with him, so give us such reality
in our devotion that our lives too may testify that we
dwell with thee, through the power of Christ. *Amen*

Read: *Matthew 6:1-13   The prayer*

O God, how often have we prayed for the coming of thy kingdom; yet when it has sought to come through us, we have barred the way; we have wanted it, without, in others, but not in our own hearts. We feel it is we who stand between man's need and thee; between ourselves and what we might be; and we have no trust in our own strength, or loyalty, or courage. O give us to love thy will, and seek thy kingdom first of all, through Christ. *Amen*

Read: *Matthew 6:24-34   The kingdom first*

Theme Three: Have Life More Abundantly

40 POWER IN GOD'S SPIRIT

Send thy Holy Spirit, O God, into our hearts, that he may direct and rule us unto all truth, through Jesus Christ our Lord. *Amen*

Read: *John 16:7-14   The Spirit promised*

O Chalice of fire that was poured on the apostles of old in the upper room, thou Holy Spirit of God: guide us with thy heavenly wisdom. Strengthen our arms as we lift hands of prayer to God in heaven, who livest and reignest with the Father and the Son, God for ever. *Amen*

Read: *Acts 2:1-7   His presence felt*

Almighty God, whose Son Jesus Christ came to cast fire upon the earth; grant that by the prayers of thy faithful people a fire of burning zeal may be kindled and pass from heart to heart, that the light of thy Church may shine forth bright and clear; through the same thy Son Jesus Christ. *Amen*

Read: *Acts 2:36-47   The Church swept into being*

O thou who hast taught us that we are most truly free when we lose our wills in thine, help us to attain to this

[53]

liberty by continual surrender unto thee; through Jesus Christ our Lord. *Amen*

Read: *Romans 8:1-10, 35-39   Life in God's spirit*

Almighty God, the inspirer of prophets and apostles, and of every true and good thought and feeling in all men; we would join the Church throughout the world in thanking thee for the gift of thy Spirit by which thou hast enabled some in all ages to be the teachers and leaders of men; and we pray thee so to pour out the same Spirit on us, that we may know and understand the deep things of God, in Christ. *Amen*

Read: *I Corinthians 12:3-11   One Spirit, many gifts*

Eternal God, we come in the name and spirit of Christ to make our wills one with thine; to abandon our lonely and selfish walk for solemn communion with thee; to put an end to sin by welcoming to our hearts thy holy presence. Deeper than we have known, enter, thou Maker of our souls; clearer than we have ever seen, dawn thy glory on our sight. *Amen*

Read: *II Corinthians 4:1-18   Perplexed, not in despair*

O thou who art heroic love, kindle we pray thee in our hearts that high spirit of adventure, in which men scorn the way of safety and seek danger, rather, to do thy will. Help us to prove worthy of their brave and loving company who, at thy bidding, put everything upon the hazard, until they passed over, and all the trumpets sounded for them on the other side. Through Christ Jesus. *Amen*

Read: *Ephesians 6:10-18   The whole armor of God*

41 **THE CHRISTIAN VIRTUES**
Jesus said: Not everyone that saith unto me, Lord, Lord, shall enter into the kingdom of heaven; but he that doeth the will of my Father who is in heaven. Who-

soever shall do the will of God, the same is my brother and sister.

It is the will of God that we should endeavor to keep our bodies in health and strength, and our appetites and impulses under control, and everywhere and in all things to be temperate and pure.

[Here and after each sentence, pause for silent meditation and prayer.]

It is the will of God that we should train our minds, and be true in our thinking, and just in all our judging . . . It is the will of God that we should be honest, truthful, and upright in thought, word, and deed . . . It is the will of God that we should be diligent and faithful in our several callings, doing our daily work in all simplicity and integrity, and seeking and laboring only for the things which are just and good . . . It is the will of God that we should rule our spirits, bear with each other's infirmities, and as much as lieth in us live peaceably with all men . . . It is the will of God that we should live chiefly to be helpful to others, and not to seek only our own pleasure and gain . . . It is the will of God that we should do what we can to take away the sin and sorrow of the world, and to overcome all evil with good . . .

Grant to us, Lord, we beseech thee, the spirit to think and do always such things as are right; that we, who cannot do anything that is good without thee, may by thee be enabled to live according to thy will, through Jesus Christ our Lord. *Amen*

Read: *Matthew 5:1-12 The Beatitudes*

Our Father, we thank thee for every opportunity of making beauty or of being good; for every victory gained over ourselves; for every day when we have stood in awe and sinned not; for every night when we have communed with our own heart upon our bed and been still. Most of all we thank thee for our Lord and Savior Jesus Christ. *Amen*

Read: *Philippians 4:4-8 Think on these things*

O Father, who by the insights of our day hast shown us anew the power of thoughts buried in our inner self, the wellsprings of action in our unconscious striving: grant us such knowledge of ourselves and such vision of thy majesty, that we may become continually more like unto thee, in Christ. *Amen*

Read: *Galatians 5:16-23 Fruits of the Spirit*

Our Father, may the world not mold us today, but may we be so strong as to help mold the world: through Christ our Lord. *Amen*

Read: *Romans 12:1-21 Overcome evil with good*

Almighty God, whose word declares that we love thee only as we love our fellow men, give us vision and obedience to show what we believe by what we do. *Amen*

Read: *James 2:1-17 Action is part of faith*

We thank thee, O God, that it is hard to be a Christian, that we can be crossed and thwarted as are others, not left apart with ghostly smooth lives dead at heart. We pray that we may have something of the eternal strength that was in Christ, so that when the rains descend and the floods come, and the winds blow and beat upon our spirits, we shall not fall, because we shall have been founded upon a Rock. *Amen*

Read: *I Timothy 6:6-21 Godliness with contentment*

42 ETERNAL LIFE

Eternal and most glorious God, suffer me not so to undervalue myself as to give away my soul, thy soul, for nothing. Preserve therefore my soul, O Lord, because it belongs to thee; and preserve my body because it belongs to my soul. *Amen*

Read: *Luke 12:2-7 Life is not the body*

O thou who art the light of my soul, I thank thee for the incomparable joy of listening to thy voice within, and I know that no word of thine shall return void, however brokenly heard. Pardon the frailty of thy servant; and look upon him only as he sinks his life in Jesus, his Master and Savior. *Amen*

Read: *John 3:14-21   Conviction and immortality*

O God of our whole destiny, Lord of eternity:

Give us a sense of the eternal in our daily life;
That even in our youthful years, we may take seriously the end of life, which the world dreads or shrugs away, and which only thy Word can help us face.

Give us a sense of the eternal in our daily life;
That despite the hopelessness we may discover in the philosophy classroom, or the urbanity we may find in science, our faith may stay strong in thee, to whom all thy children belong.

Give us a sense of the eternal in our daily life;
That at times of death we may refuse sentimentality and mawkishness, pagan ceremonial, glib sympathy, or stoic unbelief, and quietly show forth our trust in thee.

Give us a sense of the eternal in our daily life;
That as our world shudders at the threat of sudden death for whole peoples, we may yet insist that the life of the soul, in integrity, counts more than that of the body.

Give us a sense of the eternal in our daily life;
That however picturesque and symbolic may be our thought of heaven and hell, we may know that reward and remorse are thy instruments, and that our God is a Father to whom every soul is precious.

Grant us, O God, so to place our confidence in thee, and so to live out our days among our fellows, that we may dwell sure and serene in a troubled time, through him who died that we may have eternal life. *Amen*

Read: *John 14:1-4   I go to prepare a place*

We thank thee, O Lord God, that though with liberal hand thou hast at all times showered thy blessings upon our human kind, yet in Jesus Christ thou hast done greater things for us than ever thou didst before:

Making home sweeter and friends dearer:
Turning sorrow into gladness and pain into the soul's victory:
Robbing death of its sting:
Robbing sin of its power:
Renewing history:
Making peace more peaceful and joy more joyful and faith and hope more secure. *Amen*

Read: *I Corinthians 15:51-58   Victory over death*

O holy and blessed Spirit of God, whose indwelling brings the gift of joy into our lives; fill us with the gladness of God, that we may rejoice in all his works, and take pleasure in all his ways; and grant that by the happiness of our lives we may commend to all men the faith of Christ, who with thee and the Father liveth and reigneth, ever, one God, world without end. *Amen*

Read: *I John 5:1-6, 12-13   In him is life*

43 LAST THINGS
Grant, O God, that in these days when old signposts are being pulled down, we may be bold in blazing new trails, but also faithful to thy lessons of the past; that we may leave a fairer, as well as a nobler, world to those who come after us, through Jesus Christ our Savior. *Amen*

Read: *Ecclesiastes 3:1-15   Only God changes not*

O Lord, who hast set before us the great hope that thy kingdom shall come on earth, and hast taught us to pray for its coming, make us ever ready to thank thee for the signs of its dawning, and to pray and work for that perfect day when thy will shall be done on earth as it is in heaven. *Amen*

Read: *Isaiah 11:1-9   The coming reign of peace*

Almighty God, give us grace that we may cast away the works of darkness, and put upon us the armor of light, now in the time of this mortal life, in which thy Son Jesus Christ came to visit us in great humility; that in the last day, when he shall come again in his glorious majesty to judge both the living and the dead, we may rise to the life immortal; through him who liveth and reigneth with thee and the Holy Spirit, now and ever. *Amen*

Read: *Daniel 7:9-14   The everlasting dominion*

Defend us, O God, from both fear and overconfidence about future days in our life, enabling us by trust and humility to work out our salvation in thee. As men about us cry, "Lo here, lo there," of thy coming, grant us perspective to live as though thou wert to come on every morrow; as men about us say, "God is dead," grant us grace to see that thou dost work in history, and that only thou canst bring about the summation of all things. So may we with confidence go about our business, living our life with thee to whom a thousand years are but as a watch in the night. Our prayer is through Him whose once appearing and whose coming again are the bounds of our faith, even Christ. *Amen*

Read: *Mark 13:21-37   No man knows the time*

The Lord bless us and keep us. The Lord make his face to shine upon us and be gracious to us. The Lord lift up his countenance upon us, and give us peace in our going out and our coming in, in our lying down and our rising up, in our labor and our leisure, in our laughter and our tears, until we come to stand before him in that day to which there is no sunset and no dawn, through Christ. *Amen*

Read: *Revelation 21:1-7   Alpha and Omega*

PART III. OUR LIFE

On the Campus

Section One: Six Litanies on College Life

44 A LITANY FOR THE COLLEGE YEAR

Almighty God, who hast granted us place and part in this school, hallow to us now this hour, when we dedicate ourselves to the life and work to which thou hast here called us:

That we may remember with gratitude the homes and schools from which we come:
We ask thy presence, O God.
That in this new life we may keep faith with those who have loved us and trusted us, and whose hopes follow us here:
We ask thy presence, O God.
That letting no man despise our youth, we may enter with good courage and constant purpose upon the tasks which await us:
We ask thy presence, O God.
From all sense of strangeness and loneliness and from the fear that we shall find no friends:
Good Lord, deliver us.
From temptations that come suddenly, and from the sins of an unguarded hour, which may mar a lifetime:
Good Lord, deliver us.
From neglect of the opportunities which are all about us, and from distrust of our power to meet the duties of each dawning day:
Good Lord, deliver us.
That the example of wise and generous men, who have gone before us here, may save us from folly and self-indulgence:
We ask thy presence, O God.
Most especially that thou wouldst show to us and to all men the ways of peace in a day darkened with the shadows of wars:
We ask thy presence, O God.

And finally we pray that by thine aid we may keep, through all the changes of our life, the joy of a clear conscience. These things, and whatsoever else thou seest needful and right for us, we ask in the name of Christ, whom not having seen we love. *Amen*

45 A LITANY FOR HIGHER EDUCATION

O God of truth, ever beckoning man to loftier understanding and deeper wisdom, we seek thy will and implore thy grace for all who share the life of college, school, and university in our time; knowing that unless thou build amongst us, we labor in vain who teach and learn.

For men and women who teach, that they come together to bring fire and vision to a common task, knowing one field yet eager to relate it to all others, just in their academic demands yet seeing each student as a child of God, fitted to teach not only by great learning but by great faith in human kind and in thee;

In them and in us, O God, kindle thy saving truth.
(A pause to remember specific persons)

For deans and presidents, trustees and business aides, and all others who point the way for higher learning in our day, that their concern be not mainly budgets and buildings and prestige, but men and women freed into thy whole will, aroused to serve the common need;

In them and in us, O God, kindle thy saving truth.
(A pause to remember specific persons)

For janitors and maids, for cooks and keepers of the grounds, for those who wash our dishes and tend our fires, and for the host of other workers and suppliers whose faithfulness ministers to our common life;

In them and in us, O God, kindle thy saving truth.
(A pause to remember specific persons)

For parents and givers of scholarships, who send and support students in higher learning, that they seek for them not merely more income, nor social acceptance, nor glory of family or of donor, but rather hope for new breadth of intelligence, the spirit made whole, and high Christian mission in life;

In them and in us, O God, kindle thy saving truth.

(A pause to remember specific persons)

For students themselves, that their bewilderment may be brief, their perspective constantly enlarged, their minds and spirits alert both to all that classroom and campus mean, and to all that thou canst mean in their lives;

In them and in us, O God, kindle thy saving truth.

(A pause to remember specific persons)

For every member of this goodly academic fellowship, and for all who maintain us by their gifts or the daily toil of their hands, that with them we may be aware of thy Holy Spirit leading us into all truth, and one by one may grasp here thy special intention for all our learning and striving;

In them and in us, O God, kindle thy saving truth.

(A pause to remember specific persons)

We know, O heavenly Father, that what is called higher education is but the willing and planning of many men and women, each sought by thy great love. Grant that we who would earnestly serve thee may witness in their midst to the reality of thy gospel as shown forth in Christ Jesus. *Amen*

46 A LITANY FOR FAITHFULNESS ON CAMPUS

Eternal God, we praise and glorify thee, we proclaim joy before thee, for thy manifest blessings in this community of academic study:

For the expectation of good which brought us here, with the hopes and intentions of those who hold dear our destiny;

We thank thee from our hearts, O Lord.

For sound learning and exciting truth we may find here, enlarging our acquaintance with ourselves, thy world, and thee;

We thank thee from our hearts, O Lord.

[65]

For classes and books, assignments and examinations, all means of disciplining our minds and releasing them into new freedom;

We thank thee from our hearts, O Lord.

For teachers and counselors, deans and coaches, librarians and masters of research, and all others whose sharing of themselves shares also great truth;

We thank thee from our hearts, O Lord.

For Christian roots in all our learning, for the Church in campus life, for worship and prayer and Christian discipline among faculty and students;

We thank thee from our hearts, O Lord.

(Pause here)

Our prayer and our caring, O God, hold up to thee:
All students or faculty who feel alone, confused, put aside, or haunted with unreality and futility in their work, and who need thee as Father and us as brother or sister or friend.

Our prayer and our caring, O God, hold up to thee:
Young people who seeking emancipation have entered a new thralldom to unworthy thinking or behaving, now obedient to group ways which they would not at the first have chosen.

Our prayer and our caring, O God, hold up to thee:
Those who seek to pray and cannot, seek to live by thy Word yet find it closed to them, seek to control their appetites but are controlled by them, seek to use their minds to the fullest but find they cannot study.

Our prayer and our caring, O God, hold up to thee:
Those about us who, finding destroyed the faulty foundation of their Christian faith, disavow it or grope in disillusion for some great purpose to take its place in their lives.

Our prayer and our caring, O God, hold up to thee:
Leaders of campus spiritual life among students or faculty, that they may be strong, quick-thinking, never apologetic and never dull, brave to declare Christian truth amid the attractions of materialism and the eager preoccupations of secular life.

O thou whom the people called Teacher, knowledge of whose truth has set men at liberty in every generation,

grant us the grace to be faithful when we are surrounded
with likable unbelief, the grace to be trustful among
genteel scoffers, the staying power of Christian commitment even when doubt seems most reasonable. So may we
endure as seeing him who is invisible, even our strong
Savior Jesus Christ. *Amen*

47 AN ACT OF INTERCESSION FOR STUDENTS OF THE WHOLE WORLD

*[A moment of silence should be left between each peti-
tion, as well as the longer silences indicated.]*

Let us pray for the students of the whole world. For
those who are persecuted and imprisoned for their
faith . . .
For those who live in constant fear . . .
For those who are suffering hardship in consequence of
war and its effects . . .
For those who are ill . . .
For those who are hungry or cold . . .
For those who are in despair at the collapse of false
hopes.

(Silence)

Let us pray for those who are in authority, that they
may know the ultimate authority of Christ . . .
For those who are blinded by this world's success, that
they may come to know the love of God . . .
For those who are lonely, that they may find comfort
in the gospel.

(Silence)

Let us pray for those in revolutionary situations, that
they may confess their faith in the hour of trial and
that they may show forth a true picture of a community in Christ . . .
For those in newly independent countries, that they may
seize with zeal the great opportunities open to them
to bring their people closer to Christ . . .
For those who have war raging in their countries, that
they may be abundantly comforted in the face of

all terrors surrounding them, and thereby be strengthened to comfort others by word and deed.

(Silence)

Let us pray for those of us who find our work too difficult . . .

For those who do not give of their best in their work . . .

For those who are oppressed by the fear of failure in examinations . . .

For those who are perplexed and cast down by the struggle to understand the world in which they live.

(Silence)

Let us pray for those whose work is a joy to them, that they may be strengthened and enabled to communicate their joy to others . . .

For those who are engaged in the work of research and discovery, that their minds may be enlightened continually to see more of thy glory . . .

For those who are active in the life of the student community, that their influence may be for good.

(Silence)

Let us pray to God for all who teach and have the care of students in all educational institutions.

For those who work under great difficulties of time and lack of material . . .

For those who find hostility, misunderstanding, and rivalry among their colleagues.

(Silence)

Let us pray for those of us who distort the truth in the interests of false ideologies . . .

For those who are presumptuous, bitter, or indifferent, that they may come to unite with others in mutual respect and Christian love . . .

For those who have a vision of their responsibility, that they may be given the wisdom and strength to discharge it effectively.

(Silence)

Let us pray to God for the student Christian groups throughout the world, that they may be living, worshiping, and witnessing communities in the universities and schools of the world . . .

For the officers and staff of the World's Student Christian Federation, and of all national movements . . .

For student chaplains and all Christian student workers . . .
For all committees of groups in each college . . .
For every member of the Federation throughout the
world . . .
For all seekers after truth associated with Christian
groups, that their minds may be enlightened, and
their wills strengthened to follow the truth disclosed.
(Silence)
The God of hope fill us with all joy and peace in believing, that we may abound in hope, in the power of
the Holy Spirit. *Amen*

48 A MEDITATION ON RELEVANCE IN OUR
GENERATION

*"Then the righteous will answer him, 'Lord, when
did we see thee hungry and feed thee, or thirsty and give
thee drink? And when did we see thee a stranger and
welcome thee, or naked and clothe thee? And when did
we see thee sick or in prison and visit thee?' And the
King will answer them, 'Truly, I say to you, as you did
it to one of the least of these my brethren, you did it
to me.' Then he will say to those at his left hand, 'Depart from me, you cursed, into the eternal fire prepared
for the devil and his angels; for I was hungry and you
gave me no food, I was thirsty and you gave me no drink,
I was a stranger and you did not welcome me, naked
and you did not clothe me, sick and in prison and you
did not visit me.' Then they also will answer, 'Lord,
when did we see thee hungry or thirsty or a stranger or
naked or sick or in prison, and did not minister to thee?'
Then he will answer them, 'Truly, I say to you, as you
did it not to one of the least of these, you did it not to
me.'"* (Matthew 25:37-45)

Lord, keep us from being so cloistered during these
school years that we become educated to close our eyes
to need about us, trained to believe that the learned are
excused from human struggle, taught that men's wants
are met only by agencies or national programs or im-

personal public goodwill. Rather, may our studies in every field make us more deeply aware of the tragic necessities of history, the responsibility of those with special privilege, and the glory of giving our lives where the battle for justice is strongest. Thus may it be, O God, that when thou judgest what we have done and left undone, we may be found to have a true appraisal of ourselves, and worthy dependence upon the mediation of Christ our Savior. *Amen*

"You have heard that it was said, 'An eye for an eye and a tooth for a tooth.' But I say to you, Do not resist one who is evil. But if anyone strikes you on the right cheek, turn to him the other also; and if anyone would sue you and take your coat, let him have your cloak as well; and if anyone forces you to go one mile, go with him two miles." (Matthew 5:38-41)

O Master, too often we cast aside thy Word, to meet violence with violence, or worse, with craven cowardice, wounding the Lord Christ in the house of his friends. Yet thou dost lay upon us, as those who study wisdom, the poignant task of rediscovering Christ's way of love in this age, between war and appeasement, else we perish. Grant us a new resourcefulness in finding that way, together with a new insistent demand that war must cease and all God's people be one. May all our learning serve that holy purpose in thee. *Amen*

And as he was setting out on his journey, a man ran up and knelt before him, and asked him, "Good teacher, what must I do to inherit eternal life?" And Jesus said to him, "Why do you call me good? No one is good but God alone. You know the commandments: 'Do not kill, Do not commit adultery, Do not steal, Do not bear false witness, Do not defraud, Honor your father and mother.' " And he said to him, "Teacher, all these I have observed from my youth." And Jesus looking upon him loved him, and said to him, "You lack one thing: go sell all that you have, and give it to the poor, and you will have treasure in heaven; and come, follow me." At that saying his countenance fell, and he went away sorrowful; for he had great possessions. (Mark 10:17-22)

What must we do, O God, to inherit eternal life? When thou dost ask for more than we are willing to give, again and again we refuse—and go away grieved, for we have great possessions. O show us thy Son, who as he looks at us loves us, seeking our whole heart for his service! Then, O God, we shall at last surrender to thee

Our career, long-planned, stretching ahead to "success";
Our desire for popularity and power, on campus and in the world;
Our self-gratification in weakness, which we love;
Our seeking for money and all it enables us to have.

Enable us to dedicate all these to thee, our lives being remade in unexpected power and adventure because we have called thee Lord and done what thou dost command, in Christ. *Amen*

Now there was a man of the Pharisees, named Nicodemus, a ruler of the Jews. This man came to Jesus by night and said to him, "Rabbi, we know that you are a teacher come from God; for no one can do these signs that you do, unless God is with him." Jesus answered him, "Truly, truly, I say to you, unless one is born anew, he cannot see the kingdom of God." Nicodemus said to him, "How can a man be born when he is old? Can he enter a second time into his mother's womb and be born?" Jesus answered, "Truly, truly, I say to you, unless one is born of water and the Spirit, he cannot enter the kingdom of God. That which is born of the flesh is flesh, and that which is born of the Spirit is spirit."
(John 3:1-8)

Blessed God, make us aware through all our study that man is not saved by training his mind nor by new political or economic answers, nor yet by recognizing all his hidden fears and repressions; but rather by being reborn in thee. When we are tempted to believe, O God, that all reality is circled around by our little laboratory or by human relationships, lift our eyes to see thy Spirit at work in the world, reaching down into the depths of being, whispering to man that he is born of thee and can truly live only in thee, baptizing man with fire, that he may grasp his whole destiny. Grant us this rebirth in ourselves, and give us grace to declare it by word and life, to thy greater glory. *Amen*

"Now after a long time the master of those servants came and settled accounts with them. And he who had received the five talents came forward, bringing five talents more, saying, 'Master, you delivered to me five talents; here I have made five talents more.' His master said to him, 'Well done, good and faithful servant; you have been faithful over a little, I will set you over much; enter into the joy of your master.' And he also who had the two talents came forward, saying, 'Master, you delivered to me two talents; here I have made two talents more.' His master said to him, 'Well done, good and faithful servant; you have been faithful over a little, I will set you over much; enter into the joy of your master.' He also who had received the one talent came forward, saying, 'Master, I knew you to be a hard man, reaping where you did not sow, and gathering where you did not winnow; so I was afraid, and I went and hid your talent in the ground. Here you have what is yours.' But his master answered him, 'You wicked and slothful servant! You knew that I reap where I have not sowed, and gather where I have not winnowed? Then you ought to have invested my money with the bankers, and at my coming I should have received what was my own with interest. So take the talent from him, and give it to him who has the ten talents.'" (Matthew 25:19-28)

O Lord, thou hast given us much, and we tremble to realize that of us thou dost expect much again. May we who, by thy blessing, have shared life in college or school take our responsibility seriously to lead, to inspire, to sacrifice, to obey thy commandments with intelligence and skill. So do thou make our academic courses an introduction into life, and our life an introduction for others into the fuller life which is found only in thee, through Christ. *Amen*

49 A LITANY OF DEDICATION FOR STUDENTS

Remembering in this hour the needs of men and women—ourselves, and others—and looking to God for strength to make real those of our ideals which are in accord with him:

We dedicate ourselves

To a daily effort toward understanding God's way, through Bible study, prayer, corporate worship, and careful thought;

To continued intellectual and spiritual growth in the meaning and implications of Christian faith, by reading, conversation, and reflection;

To participation in the work of the Church Universal, through our own denomination and congregation.

Remembering that we have this treasure in earthen vessels, and with deep humility, nevertheless:

We dedicate ourselves

To the sharing of this faith and the winning of others to active allegiance, by the contagion of earnest living and by the persuasion of the spoken word;

To the uprooting of small evils, which are the source of greater evils, in our own lives and in our immediate group in college life.

Believing that "blessed are they that mourn," when so many of those whom Jesus called our neighbors are in deep distress:

We dedicate ourselves

To the cultivation of an abiding sensitiveness to great social wrongs, and a lasting refusal to become comfortably complaisant;

To the better understanding of complex social patterns which often make men of goodwill partners in wrong and injustice;

To the faithful performance of commonplace and routine duties, without the thrill of great excitement or the impulsion of pride in being the greatest;

To the maintenance of whatever uplift of spirit has been achieved in Christian fellowship, hardening high inspiration into the tough fiber of daily effort;

[73]

To the fullest use of our student Christian movement
as an effective linking of our group with the larger
company of Christian students here and everywhere;
To the discovery of, or continuance in, a life occupation
which will be our primary and major expression of
faith.
In all these ways, to the service and adoration of Jesus
Christ, whom we joyfully hail as Lord and Master, truly
God and truly man, in gratitude and love:

We dedicate ourselves. Amen

Section Two: Prayers on the Meaning of Study

50 O God, we thank thee for burning ideas that take
lodgment in our minds, insistent to be heard. Lord, unto
thee would we dedicate the voyages of our seeking minds.
We would yield to thee the dim gropings of our spirits, the
unfathomed aspirations of our truest selves, beseeching
thee to fashion them into a living harmony with thy
purposes. And this we ask for Jesus Christ's sake. *Amen*

51 God of all wisdom, thrust thou me into a life-
long quest of great ideas.
Save me from easy contentment with small thoughts
whose cost is little and whose rewards are slight.
Stir within me some inward and holy passion for the
mighty thoughts that, costing all, reward the soul
with all.
Through great books quicken me with the growing-pains
of the mind.
Teach me the thrill and the enlargement that are found
in keeping pace with the great minds of the ages.
Grant me a divine grace in the ability to ask questions,
sharp questions that cut deep and divide truth from
error.

Spare me the inner defeat of easy answers.

Enlarge me by the wisdom that has come down from my
     fathers. Grant me as well the courage to outgrow it
     as they outgrew what had come down to them.

Cleanse me of small spites, purge my soul of puny
     hatreds, sweep my heart of paralyzing bitterness
     through the ennobling power of great ideas.

In the name of him who is the truth. *Amen*

52 Grant, O Lord, to all teachers and students, to
know that which is worth knowing, to love that which
is worth loving, to praise that which pleaseth thee most,
and to dislike whatsoever is evil in thine eyes. Grant us
with true judgment to distinguish things that differ, and
above all to search out and to do what is well-pleasing
to thee, through Jesus Christ our Lord. *Amen*

53 God, who hast given us power to reason, exper-
iment, and discover, teach us to use these gifts aright.
Help us to know our limitations lest, claiming a mo-
nopoly of the truth, we become proud of our intellect and
vain in our imaginations, through Jesus Christ our Lord.
Amen

54 Father, who hast blessed this school for a place
of faith and fruitful study: grant us likewise in it so
to learn truth as to bear its light along our ways, and so
to learn Christ as ever to be found in him, who liveth
and reigneth with thee and the Holy Spirit, one God,
world without end. *Amen*

55 Our heavenly Father, give us the courage and insight to seek out the defects in the way we think and live today. Make us intelligently critical of all mere inherited, conventional religion, as also of the affirmations and claims of science and education and social service. Keep us from holding onto pious error when greater truth has been discovered. We feel that thou wilt not desert us because we think in different ways and dare to question old customs and dogmas. We have no fear of faith broken by open eyes and consecrated hearts. Help us in our modern quest, and make us as good followers of thy Son in our day as were the men of old. In Jesus' name we pray. *Amen*

56 Almighty and most merciful Father, who hast graciously supplied me with new conveniences for study, grant that I may use thy gifts to thy glory. Forgive me the time misspent, relieve my perplexities, strengthen my resolution, and enable me to do my duty with vigor and constancy; and when the fears and hopes, and pains and pleasures of this life shall have an end, receive me to the everlasting happiness, for the sake of Jesus Christ our Lord. *Amen*

57 O God, Holy Spirit, the source of all truth, enlighten with thy wisdom those who teach and those who learn, that rejoicing in the knowledge of thy truth, they may worship thee and serve thee from generation to generation, through Jesus Christ our Lord. *Amen*

58 We give thee thanks, O God, for the harvest of knowledge, patiently gathered over long years by on-going generations of scholars, and now laid up for the needs of mankind in our universities and colleges. For the increasing mastery of special skills, for victory over ills which man has suffered through his ignorance, for confidence in the reliable order of nature, for the wisdom which long experience adds to much learning, for ever-new light falling on old mysteries, as for all the joys of our part and portion in man's unconquerable mind: we give thee thanks. *Amen*

59 As seekers after the truth, O God, we confess the hesitancy and inconstancy which hinder us in our search. That which we find is often unwelcome and uncomfort-able; we evade the truth and reassure ourselves by self-deception, clinging to old familiar errors or cherishing the lie in the soul. The problems of our time are be-wildering; we take refuge in evasion and indifference. Speak then, O God, to our fugitive souls, to renew both our candor and our courage. In Christ. *Amen*

60 Grant, O Lord, we pray thee, that as we seek for truth we may find that the search leads us to thyself. Give us courage to seek honestly and reverence to seek humbly; and when our minds are perplexed, and we can-not find thee, give us patience to go on with our daily duties, through Jesus Christ our Lord. *Amen*

61 *Resolutions for a student's day:*

Not to be dilatory in beginning the day's main work.

To neglect no task; to observe the proportion of tasks.

Not to murmur at the press of duties or shortness of time, but to buy up time all round.

Not to magnify responsibilities by seeming to suffer under them, but to treat all as liberties and gladnesses.

Not to call attention to crowded work or petty fatigues, or trivial experiences.

To learn how unintentionally forbidding and depressing our tone and look can be if we lack inner peace.

Before censuring anyone, to obtain from God a real love for him or her.

To seek no favor, no compassion; to deserve but not to ask for tenderness.

To bear blame rather than share or transmit it.

Not to let the affection and regard of others be an unpaid debt.

62 Deliver us, O God, from following the fashions of the day in our thinking. Save us from the worship of power, whether power over nature or power over men; save us from the worship of science, and grant that giving thee thanks for the skill of the scientist, we may be preserved from the abuse of his discoveries. Help us never to confuse any creature with the Creator, or man with God. May we acknowledge man's reason as thy gift and, being freed from all false hopes and misplaced trust, find in thee our hope and our salvation, through Jesus Christ our Lord. *Amen*

63 O thou who art the Source and Ground of all truth, thou Light of lights, who hast opened the minds of men to discern the things that are, guide me today, I beseech thee, in my hours of reading. Give me grace to choose the right books and to read them in the right way. Give me wisdom to abstain as well as to persevere. Let the Bible have proper place; and grant that as I read I may be alive to the stirrings of thy Holy Spirit in my soul. *Amen*

64   O thou Giver of wisdom and skill, we confess that we have scorned those who labor mainly with their hands; we have prided ourselves upon our superior intellect, and have looked down upon the skilled hands and the honest labor of those who also maintain the fabric of the world, and in whose handicraft is their prayer. Take from us all that makes us unworthy of our privileges, and help us to remember that we are able to pursue our studies only because others perform their labors, through Jesus Christ our Lord. *Amen*

65   O God, we pray thee to send thy blessing upon this school and grant that by the help of thy Holy Spirit we may strive with one heart and one mind to make this a place more and more pleasing to thee, for the honor and glory of thy Son our Savior, Jesus Christ. *Amen*

66   Our Father, we thank thee for such strength of body, intelligence of mind, kindness of heart, and love for thee as thou hast given us, and we pray that the gift that is within us may not be lost through disuse nor destroyed through misuse, but developed in these days for greater service to the world and to thy Kingdom. In Jesus' name. *Amen*

67 O Lord Jesus Christ, who on thy cross didst overcome all the powers of darkness, guide all men who in seeking knowledge acquire power which can be used for good or evil purposes. Help them to bear their responsibility, and in awe to recognize their stewardship. *Amen*

68 Lord, we thank thee for all the wisdom of the past; for the devoted labors of sages and thinkers who have prized truth above all things; for the discipline of clear thinking, and the dissipation of confusion and prejudice. Grant us, we pray thee, the love of truth for Christ's sake; teach us to care more for truth than for systems, or for skill in debate; and give us the grace and patience to keep open those questions which philosophy cannot answer. In Christ. *Amen*

69 *We would worship God with minds transformed by his renewing:*
That we lack not honesty in doubts and perplexity.
That we lack not accuracy in scholarship and research.
That we may collaborate with others in the search for truth, and may never for popularity or riches turn aside from our task.

We would worship God in proving what is his will, in doing what is good and acceptable and perfect in his sight:

[80]

That we may bring all our studies under the good hand of God.

That we may see all things in relation to God, the giver of all truth.

That we may not rest in contemplation of the truth, but may perform it.

That we may bring all thoughts and imaginations into captivity to Christ.

Section Three: Prayers on the Daily Round

70 FOR ATHLETICS AND SPORT

God of all good strength, increase in these days our control and enjoyment of our bodies, with hard-won skill of muscle and mind and eye, the discipline of unselfish teamwork, and honest striving to win the game; that in our lives we may learn to run the race for the prize of eternal life, in Christ. *Amen*

O Lord, grant us the best rewards in all our contests of strength and skill. Deliver us from vainglory and egoism, from spite and the harboring of any grudge, from playing hard to win only for an advantage of pride or subsidy. Make us thoughtful winners and gracious losers. Keep our great games between schools from becoming orgies, our rivalries from becoming obsessions. Enable us to be doers, not always mere spectators, in athletics and in life. So may we share the clean joy of athletes in all the ages. *Amen*

O God, who hast made a world where struggle brings strength but indolence leads to weakness, we thank thee for those contests which challenge our best in mind and muscle. Grant us to grow in strength of body and keenness of mind through the games in which we participate, and as we go onto the field of life, help us to remember that what is hardest may be most rewarding, and that the goal which is most distant may be most glorious. In Jesus' name. *Amen*

O thou whose Son faced every ordeal with deep strength, help us to rid ourselves of all bodily fears; enable us to play our games skillfully, courageously, and with all our might, and so temper our courage that when the hour of real peril comes we may stand firm and faithful if need be even unto death, through Jesus Christ our Lord. *Amen*

71 **ON BEING A GOOD ROOMMATE**

Give us grace, O God, to cherish the friendship of those with whom we share our living; in the blessed friction of learning mutual respect, in the matching of moods and the accommodating of habits, in the opportunity for witness and the sharing of prayer; grant us new evidence how one heart may fortify another, and both be drawn nearer to thee in Christ. *Amen*

72 **ON CHOOSING FRIENDS**

O God, as we like our friends to value us, grant that our desire for popularity may never lead us into the weakness and cowardice of condoning what we should condemn, nor of caring more for what men think than for the doing of thy will. Help us to choose the hard part when necessary, and to stand by the weak, the downtrodden, and the unpopular; for the sake of Jesus Christ our Lord. *Amen*

Grant, O Lord, that we may love the unloved as did thy Son our Lord, reaching out to the unattractive and lonely, the despised and unfriendly, the difficult and resentful; and grant, O thou great Friend, that we do this not to gain followers nor to merit thanks, but because we have within us love enough and to spare, and because our life is patterned on his who came to seek and to save that which was lost. *Amen*

73 **FOR CAMPUS POLITICS**

To thee, O God, we lift the continuing contest for power among students and faculty in this community of learning: may none of us use others for our own gain; may none conceal or mislead as we seek advantage for ourselves or our friends; may our campus leadership be dedicated, unselfish, a token of Christian democracy. Grant, O holy Father, that we may be fit to govern or to choose among our fellows, because we have first been governed and chosen by thee. *Amen*

74 **AT EXAMINATION TIME**

O Lord, throughout our examinations grant us a quiet mind, a good memory, and a ready comprehension of what we have studied, and keep us ever honest in deed and in thought, for the sake of Jesus Christ our Lord. *Amen*

O God, who knowest the secrets of the heart, be with those now preparing for examinations. Help them to face their task with calmness, confidence, and courage; with wisdom, faithfulness, and honesty; that they may do justice both to themselves and to their teachers, and set forth thy glory, who thyself art wisdom and truth, and the giver of knowledge, and of every virtue and good gift in Jesus Christ our Lord. *Amen*

O God, be with me today and help me to do my best. Give me a clear mind and an honest heart. If there are things I do not know, let me not be flustered or afraid, but use to the utmost what I do know. May everything in which I have worked hard stand by me now; and if in anything I must face the results of laziness, make me resolve to work better in the days ahead. Help me to express all I know; but whether I can do that or not, grant that I may have learned something that will last, through Jesus Christ my Master. *Amen*

75 O thou, whose disciples fasted not nor were of a sad countenance, give us joy in romance and courtship, that in pure intention and in reverence for every child of thine, we may know unselfish affection and so deepen our love of thee. *Amen*

We invoke thy blessing, our Father, on all true lovers. We thank thee for the revealing power of love which divines in the one beloved the mystic beauty and glory of humanity, overcoming the selfishness of youth by the passion of self-surrender. We pray thee to make their love strong and holy, that no misunderstanding may fray the bond, and no gray disenchantment of the years may have the power to quench the heavenly light that now glows in them. May they reverence themselves and drink the cup of joy with awe. In Christ. *Amen*

O God, in the days when life seems hopeful and care-free and joyous, may we not, in our desire for freedom and fun and achievement, trifle with great forces and great principles, and thus store up for ourselves in our later years reservoirs of bitterness and remorse. May we never delude ourselves into thinking that we can have an unrestrained fling now, and then turn untouched to thy way in later life, when our desires shall have been satisfied.

O keep us from degrading or belittling the personalities of others. Help us to shun dreams and thoughts and acts which will degrade us and fill our souls with all sorts of darkness and despair. In our social and personal life may we ever keep foremost the value of integrity and respect and character.

And as we differ and grow impatient with those who are older, may we not in our revolt give ourselves over to perilous recklessness, but rather devote our talents and energies to making better character and a better world than the one in which our forebears lived. This we ask in the name of him who taught us to live abundantly and joyously and helpfully. *Amen*

76 FOR A GOOD VACATION

O God, who art the foundation of all true joys, we pray for all who leave their studies at this season to enjoy the pleasures of recreation and renewal of family ties. Sanctify to their use the rhythm of life wherein work and play alternate as day and night. May their moments of relaxation be offered to thee as a gift acceptable in thy sight, through Christ. *Amen*

Our Father, we are glad to recall the time when Jesus led his tired disciples apart into a desert place that they might rest awhile, and we are grateful for the approach of the season when we, too, may go away and find refreshment. If it be possible, may we depart with a good conscience and a clear desk, and may we come again with a reinvigorated body and an eager spirit. In his name. *Amen*

77 FOR MILITARY ASPECTS OF OUR LIFE

Good Lord, who hast set our lives in a time of war, enable us to convert to a good purpose whatever military demands are laid upon us: if we undergo training, may it strengthen our discipline and lift our ideals of teamwork and service; if we face combat, may it not wrench away our Christian sympathy nor harden our heart; if we refuse the military way, may our decision be made with insight and humility; so that whatever our response to the violence of men and nations, we may continually fight the good fight of faith, in him whose kingdom is not of this world. *Amen*

78 ON GETTING OUT OF A RUT

O blessed God, who makest all things continually new, redeem us from settling into a lifeless routine of sleeping, eating, study, and play, never raising our eyes to the adventure and glory thou dost intend for us. Keep us from being old before our time, O Lord, by showing us the unexpectedness of prayer and the daring of lives handed over to thy command: through him who risked all to show thy love. *Amen*

79 FOR THOSE WHO STUDY TOO MUCH OR TOO LITTLE

O Father, in whom there is a time for all things, we pray thee for a right view of our academic work; guard us from too much study, which warps perspective, withers friendship, and serves an unhealthy ambition or evasion; but deliver us likewise, O Lord, from too little study, which denies our right to be here, betrays our responsibility to ourselves and our school, pointing ahead to long regret or continuing laziness; help us to carry out with maturity and faithfulness all the work we are justly given to do, in Christ. *Amen*

80 FOR STEADINESS IN PRAYER

O Lord, whose Son arose before dawn to pray, even though his hours were busier than any man's: give us grace to let no day pass without prayer; enable us to remember thee again and again during the daily round, as we rise, as we eat, as we study, as we play, as we go again to our sleep; that continually we may grow in grace and in constant awareness of thy love, through Christ. *Amen*

Section Four: Campus Failings

81 FROM SNOBBERY

Guard us, O God, from all false setting of barriers in this community, from snobbery, and from feelings of condescension or inferiority, knowing that these

narrow those about us, narrow ourselves, and narrow thy
great love. Make us like him who has bidden us not to
judge our fellows but to accept them fully, and who was
the friend of rich and poor, wise and simple, cultured
and crude, lovable and unlovely; even Christ the Son of
Man. *Amen*

82 FROM CRIBBING

Defend us, O God, from the petty dishonor of
cheating, on examinations or in writing papers, in friendship or in games; not because we can be pure or perfect
in ourselves, but because in Christ thou givest us the victory when we are as honest as we can be. *Amen*

83 FROM BEING TOO SMOOTH

Almighty God, to whom a ready heart is dearer
than a ready tongue, to whom candor is more pleasing
than sophistication, redeem us from using words and
people only to our personal advantage; grant that we
may be honest with ourselves and them and thee, through
him who was full of grace and truth. *Amen*

84 FROM UNWISE DRINKING

O thou who hast called us to a godly, righteous,
and sober life, grant us such simplicity and sincerity that
we may feel no need to caricature our powers by drink-
ing; deliver us from wishing to appear to ourselves and
others as that which we are not. O God, keep us aware
in all humility that however unwilling or unwitting, we
are constantly the guide to someone weaker, to whom
our freedom may be the occasion of stumbling. Give us
grace, we pray thee, in so far as we are able, to keep

both head and conscience clear, thus honoring thee, our Maker, through Christ. *Amen*

85 ON STUDENT-FACULTY RELATIONS

Grant, O Lord, a right mutual regard between student and teacher in our midst; spare either from arrogance, suspicion, pride, enmity, or false parading of knowledge; endue both with humility, trust for each other, and such personal concern as reaches beyond course and classroom in wider Christian understanding, through him who was both learner and teacher of life. *Amen*

86 FROM WASTE AND WANTONNESS

O God, defend us from reckless spending, from destructive exuberance, from selfish celebration of personal satisfactions, and from throwing away our time and our deepest abilities; grant us a spirit continually blithe and constructive, that we may know both how to be abased and how to abound, in Christ. *Amen*

87 FROM LOSING BALANCE AMONG ACTIVITIES

O Son of Man, known at weddings and suppers and on the roads, faithful at worship, a friend in many households: enable us to weigh wisely all activities and occasions on campus. Give us such a sure sense of what is important, that we may most fruitfully allot our time to our studies, our sports, our clubs, our dating, our friends, and our Church; to the end that we may be true stewards of time and skill, through him of whom it was said that he did all things well, even Christ our Lord. *Amen*

[88]

Section Five: Prayers for Persons and Groups

88 ### FOR OUR FAMILIES

O God, who hast bidden us to honor our parents, and who by thy Son our Savior hast sanctified the life of home: bless, we beseech thee, with thy gracious protection all those who are related to me; keep them in health and safety; help me lovingly to fulfill my duty to them, and knit us closely together in love and worship of thee, through the same Jesus Christ our Lord. *Amen*

O heavenly Father, whose only-begotten Son was thankful for thy great mercies in word and deed, enable us, we beseech thee, to show our gratitude to our parents for their love, by a cheerful obedience to their wishes, and a loving thoughtfulness for their happiness, through the same Jesus Christ. *Amen*

O God, help us to keep clear the channels of understanding and affection with the older generation in our homes, with our fathers and mothers who love us but do not always understand that we are really growing up. May he who taught men long ago to say "Our Father" teach us now again to give joy as the fair return for the joy and opportunity that we receive. *Amen*

Bless, O God, all the members of our family and household, especially those who are absent from us. Preserve them waking, guard them in their going out and their coming in, free from sin and safe from danger, and when they sleep may they rest in peace; through Jesus Christ our Lord. *Amen*

89 ### FOR FACULTY MEMBERS

O Lord Jesus Christ, who didst sit lowly in the midst of the doctors, both hearing them and asking them questions; grant unto thy servants of this faculty both aptness to teach and willingness to learn thy blessed will; who livest and reignest, with the Father and the Holy Spirit, one God, world without end. *Amen*

[89]

O heavenly Father, endue with thy wisdom those who teach, and grant unto them patience in the pursuit of truth and in the imparting of it to those committed to their charge. Open their minds to see the eternal values lying behind the things of this world; and grant that both by their teaching and by their living they may bring men to a closer knowledge of thee, through Jesus Christ our Lord. *Amen*

90 FOR THOSE WHO SPECIALIZE

O God, who hast made us to know each other and thee, enable all who study here so to learn from each other and from thee, that we may attain our full stature in thy sight. Give to all specialists such a breadth of vision that they may not ignore or forget the other members of the community. Break down our intellectual divisions, so that we may all be one in our calling of study, and in the body of our Lord Jesus Christ. *Amen*

91 FOR STUDENTS FROM ABROAD

Almighty God, we pray for students from overseas who come to this country:

That they may be drawn into the fellowship of a Christian congregation;

That they may continue faithful in the practice of their religion;

That their faith may not be shaken by the irreligion of many in this country.

O Lord our God, who art in every place, and from whom no space or distance can separate us: we pray for those who are far from the home of their fathers in a strange land. Grant that they may live as faithful followers of Jesus Christ, and be living members of his body which is the Church, through the same thy Son, our Lord and Savior. *Amen*

O God the Father of all mankind, we would remember before thee the men and women who come from many lands to study on our campuses. Guide and protect them in the difficulties which beset them in their new surroundings. Keep alive in their hearts the love of all that is good in their home life, and give them also insight to appreciate and share that which is good in ours. Pardon the faults of temper and manners by which we often offend them; and grant unto us true humility, love, and patience that we may welcome them in the spirit of the Master whom we desire to serve. *Amen*

92 FOR TOWNSPEOPLE ABOUT US

O thou who didst find honor except among fellow townsmen, keep large our view of those who live near the campus but do not share its life of learning; make us aware that if they try our patience, we rather more constantly try theirs; enable the school to be spiritually a blessing to its surrounding community, raising up its students to be citizens of this campus, of this neighborhood, and of thy kingdom. *Amen*

93 FOR SERVICE WORKERS ON CAMPUS

We thank thee, Lord, for the faithfulness of those who care for this place, serve our food, and ease our life with endless daily chores; grant to them joy in what they do, and to us grace to show our thankfulness to them and thee, in Christ. *Amen*

94 FOR THOSE IN FINANCIAL HARDSHIP

O thou whose Son had not where to lay his head, keep us considerate of those in our academic fellowship who are continually under the shadow of need, whose waking hours must be always given to earning money, whose studies and pleasures are narrowed by worry over material things; in our planning and our spending, grant us simplicity and the grace of sharing, in Christ. *Amen*

95 **FOR A FRATERNITY OR CLUB**

O Lord, to whom it is good and pleasant that brethren should dwell together in unity, may thy will be done amongst those here bound by special ties of tradition and friendship; deliver us from all arrogance or unworthy clannishness, from desire for luxury or too great conformity to a pattern, from contempt of our fellows or ruthlessness in dealing with any child of God; make us grateful for a great heritage of comradeship and common purpose, and knit us deeply into the larger fellowship of all Christian souls, through him who is first among many brethren, even Christ. *Amen*

96 **FOR GRADUATES OF THIS SCHOOL**

O Father of all generations, we invoke thy blessing, and bestow our own, upon those who have studied here and gone out to their work in the world; may we understand their affection for this place, never becoming cynical about the demands they make upon it, nor about the demands we make upon them; grant them wisdom in what they seek for the school, and resourcefulness in using what was given them here; so may they and we, sharing a lasting gratitude for what has been given us here, lift up this school continually unto thee, for thy guidance and enduring grace, in Christ. *Amen*

Section Six: Student Life in the Church

97 **A LITANY FOR THE STUDENT CHRISTIAN MOVEMENT**

Eternal God, known in the trustfulness of childhood and the wisdom of old age, and to be worshiped in all the years of our lives, grant thy power and blessing to all who are students in this time, that in their faith the Church may be strong, thy kingdom sought with fresh intelligence and dedication:

For the heritage of all the centuries, that through students thou hast restored the urgency of thy gospel, in early academies and first universities, in monasteries and in mission bands, in colleges and seminaries of learning;

We are grateful, O Lord.

For the increase of education in recent generations, by which millions in college and university have been led to explore the truth, understanding more fully our world and their own lives;

We are grateful, O Lord.

For the witness, taken up scores of years ago, by the Young Men's and Women's Christian Associations on our campuses, speaking gladly and powerfully as the Church among students;

We are grateful, O Lord.

For the pouring out of thy grace among the colleges at the close of last century through the Student Volunteer Movement, calling tens of thousands to heroic service in evangelization of the world in their generation;

We are grateful, O Lord.

For the awakening of the whole Church during our own century, to follow its students to every campus with counsel and teaching, with assurance of fellowship and the sacraments of thy grace;

We are grateful, O Lord.

For the real and growing togetherness of our Christian programs among students, wrought by years of prayer and planning, and by selfless, tireless devotion of many men and women;

We are grateful, O Lord.

For the richness and variety of student Christian activity: for the great conferences which lift thousands; for retreats and quiet circles where thy Word is cherished by the few; for student gatherings by lake or mountainside, renewing thy Church season after season in worship, discussion, and friendship; for the daily round in campus groups and foundations, offering forth thy truth steadily among our fellow students;

We are grateful, O Lord.

[93]

For older leaders of Christian student life, men and women who with resourcefulness and devotion, often with small pay and recognition, mediate thy truth and love to a demanding generation;
We are grateful, O Lord.

That our witness as Christians amid the wistfulness and cynicism of our colleagues has been halfhearted and embarrassed,
Forgive us, O God.
That the appeals of eloquent speakers, the startling truths found in discussion, and the promptings of thy Spirit in worship have stirred our hearts too little, and too briefly amended our living,
Forgive us, O God.
That efforts to unite Christian denominations and traditions on campus have been small, and have thus denied the wholeness of thy gospel before the world,
Forgive us, O God.
That we are often so overwhelmed with committees and plans and recreation that the one thing needful, our sharing the power of thy Word, is crowded out of our Christian program,
Forgive us, O God.

To kindle in the whole student Christian movement a historic renewal of thy truth and its revolutionary meaning in human affairs,
Convert and convince us, O Lord.
To knit up the relation of students with faculty so that those who teach and those who sit in class may share together a common ministry of thy grace,
Convert and convince us, O Lord.
To search out for thy service in the Church and in every calling the keenest and most daring men and women in our schools, summoning them forth to change the world according to thy command,
Convert and convince us, O Lord.
To support and encourage all our leaders, that they may ably guide the larger destiny and effectiveness of thy Church's work among students everywhere,
Convert and convince us, O Lord.

Blessed God, keep us aware that we are the Church of tomorrow, preparing now on campus to make its witness exciting or insipid, world shaking or tame, the salvation of all mankind or the comfortable assurance of the privileged. Do thou so move us with thy might, that the nation-wide and world-wide movement of Christian students in this day may again glorify thee and renew the dynamic witness of thy Church. *Amen*

A LITANY FOR THE WORLD'S STUDENT CHRISTIAN FEDERATION

98 Let us pray for the World's Student Christian Federation, and for all the national movements which compose it:

That through the work of the Federation the students of many lands may be drawn nearer to one another, that so the barriers of ignorance and prejudice may be broken down, and the foundation laid of understanding and goodwill on which alone the global unity of nations can be built;

Quicken this fellowship, O God.

That we may be swift to grasp the opportunities offered us in the Federation, through friendships made with students of other lands at conferences and in college, through study and travel, through lectures and discussions;

Quicken this fellowship, O God.

That we may be faithful in thought and prayer for each other; that we may never let our own concerns and difficulties make us forgetful of the needs of other Movements;

Quicken this fellowship, O God.

That alike in Christian and non-Christian countries Christ may be so lifted up that he may draw all men unto himself;

Quicken this fellowship, O God.

Let us pray for the officers and committees of the Federation, whether in Geneva or traveling among the colleges at this time; for the leaders of the various national Movements, and for all their members.

(A moment of silence)

Let us remember especially the students who have left their homes to study in other lands, the foreign students in our own country, in Britain, in Europe, and on other continents:

(A moment of silence)

That through all the difficulties which they have to face they may feel thy guiding and sustaining hand;

Quicken this fellowship, O God.

That they may meet with courtesy and kindliness in every land to which they go, that through the friendships thus formed, the East and the West, the North and the South may share with each other all that is best in their inheritance;

Quicken this fellowship, O God, and bless us continually as thy children, in Christ our Lord. Amen

99 FOR CHRIST'S CHURCH ON CAMPUS

Almighty God, reverence for whom is the beginning of wisdom, keep us alive to the needs and possibilities of thy Church among those who teach and learn; grant to her leaders, ordained and unordained, special grace to believe, courage to declare, skill to interpret, and steadiness to endure; that the company of Christians in this place may be numbered surely among those who know thee and serve thy kingdom with a whole heart, through our Lord Jesus Christ. *Amen*

Vocation and Careers

Section One: Litanies and Meditations

100   A LITANY ON CHRISTIAN VOCATION

O Lord of glory, who carriest the stars in their timeless orbits, and sustainest all matter and mind in their appointed working, we give thee thanks and praise, that thou dost yet also claim each of us for thyself in an eternal purpose.

For the mystery of creation, wherein thou didst make man for fellowship with thyself,
We thank thee with a whole heart, O God.
For the variety of man's gifts and enthusiasms, each of us differing uniquely, formed with a special intention to fulfill in thee,
We thank thee with a whole heart, O God.
For the ways by which thou dost reveal thy will to our minds, pointing us forward by tokens of our physical endowments, our family, our opportunities and education and experience,
We thank thee with a whole heart, O God.
For the plentiful reward given to live our lives unto thee, in satisfactions, friendships, and the exaltation of co-operating with thee in thy holy purpose,
We thank thee with a whole heart, O God.
For the fellowship of thy Church, the Body of Christ thy Son, within whose far-flung membership are men and women serving thee in every worthy task, making these their ministries of thy blessed kingdom,
We thank thee with a whole heart, O God.
(Pause)
Aware of the want and wistfulness all about us, of the poverty of soul in millions who lack any vision of thy glory, any true perspective of their work,
We seek our work and witness in thee, Lord.
Aware that all who seek to follow thy way among the

[97]

ways of men must expect misunderstanding and scorn, temptations to hypocrisy, perplexities, and hard decisions,

We seek our work and witness in thee, Lord.

Aware of thy need for workers in pulpit and parish, in faraway mission and nearby slum, and in every outreach of thy Church, yet also in every lay task and responsibility,

We seek our work and witness in thee, Lord.

Aware of the summons brought by thy kingdom in every calling, every business and school, every shop and trade, for convinced apostles of the gospel of Christ,

We seek our work and witness in thee, Lord.

Aware that as we do seek first thy kingdom and thy righteousness, our Master promises that all other needful things shall be added unto us,

We seek our work and witness in thee, Lord.

(Pause)

To help us use every means for discovering thy purpose for us, thy timeless intention for our lives,

Grant us thy quickening grace.

To make us sensitive to all that thy holy Word brings for our counsel as we read its pages and ponder its meanings,

Grant us thy quickening grace.

To enable us to employ every human gift of analysis and guidance, uncovering in us that which has been known to thee but not to ourselves,

Grant us thy quickening grace.

To show us through our studies, our friendships, our family, and our vacation experiences what lifework thou wouldst have us do,

Grant us thy quickening grace.

To bring us through our larger calling as redeemed believers, lifted from sinfulness to joy in Christ, to realize how every useful task may likewise be reclaimed for thy service,

Grant us thy quickening grace.

O Gracious God, who hast appointed us to live for thee in a time when the gospel is true adventure for those who dedicate themselves to its demand and its joy, we pray thee to bring us completely to that point of daring where human need and divine purpose meet, that we may be part of that mighty Incarnation whereby thou dost yet show thyself a dweller among men, renewing vision for all our work, and bringing eternal life amid the whole round of duty, in Christ Jesus our Lord. *Amen*

101 AN ACT FOR KNOWING GOD'S WILL

Almighty God, whose truth alone can make us free, and who hast bidden each of us to take up some special task in thy kingdom, keep us alert to thy commands and persuasions, eager to carry out the whole duty thou dost set for us, that the work of our hands may be established in thee, through Christ. *Amen*

Jesus said: Seek ye first the kingdom of God and his righteousness and all these things shall be added unto you.

It is the will of God:

To gather together in one all things in Christ, both which are in heaven and which are on earth.

That we should show forth his praises who called us out of the darkness into his marvelous light.

That we should believe in him and love him with all our heart, with all our mind, with all our soul, and with all our strength.

That we should worship him and put our whole trust in him all the days of our life.

Lord, we believe; help thou our unbelief.

(Pause)

Jesus said: Ye are the salt of the earth, but if the salt hath lost its savor, wherewith shall it be salted? Ye are the light of the world.

It is the will of God:

That our light should so shine before men that they may see our good works and glorify our Father in heaven.

That speaking the truth in love, we should grow up together in all things unto him, who is the head of the Body, even Christ.

That we should train our minds to be true in our thinking and just in all our judging.

That we should be honest, truthful, and upright in thought, word, and deed.

That we should be diligent and faithful in our several callings, doing our daily work in all simplicity and integrity, and laboring only for the things which are just and good.

> Lord, we believe; help thou our unbelief.

(Pause)

> Jesus said: Not everyone that saith unto me, Lord, Lord, shall enter into the kingdom of heaven; but he that doeth the will of my Father who is in heaven. Whosoever shall do the will of God, the same is my brother and sister.

It is the will of God:

That we should rule our spirits, bear with each other's infirmities, and as much as lieth in us live peaceably with all men.

That we should live chiefly to minister to others' needs and not to seek only our own pleasure and gain.

That we should do what we can to take away the sin and sorrow of the world and to overcome evil with good.

That we should not be anxious for the morrow, nor for our life what we shall eat or what we shall drink, nor for the body what we shall put on.

> Lord, we believe; help thou our unbelief.

(Pause)

Grant to us, Lord, we beseech thee, the spirit to think and do always such things as are right; that we, who cannot do anything that is good without thee, may by thee be enabled to live according to thy will; through Jesus Christ our Lord. Amen

102 A LITANY FOR ALL WORKERS

O God, who hast made us a royal priesthood, that we might offer unto thee prayer and intercession for all sorts and conditions of men, hear us as we pray:

For all who toil in the burden and the heat of the day, that they may enjoy the rewards of their industry, that they may not be defrauded of their due, and that we may never cease to be mindful of our debt to them, remembering with gratitude the multitude of services which must be performed to make our life tolerable.

We pray thy grace and pledge our concern, O God.
For those who have authority and power over their fellow men, that they may not use it for selfish advantage, but be guided to do justice and to love mercy:

We pray thy grace and pledge our concern, O God.
For those who have been worsted in the battles of life, whether by the inhumanity of their fellows, their own limitations, or the fickleness of fortune, that they may contend against injustice without bitterness, overcome their own weakness with diligence, and learn how to accept what cannot be altered with patience:

We pray thy grace and pledge our concern, O God.
For the rulers of the nations that they may act wisely and without pride, may seek to promote peace among the peoples and establish justice in our common life:

We pray thy grace and pledge our concern, O God.
For teachers and ministers of the word, for artists and interpreters of our spiritual life, that they may rightly divine the word of truth, and not be tempted by pride or greed or any ignoble passion to corrupt the truth to which they are committed:

We pray thy grace and pledge our concern, O God.
For prophets and seers and saints, who awaken us from our sloth, that they may continue to hold their torches high in a world darkened by prejudice and sin, and ever be obedient to the heavenly vision:

We pray thy grace and pledge our concern, O God.

O Lord, who hast bound us together in this bundle of life, give us grace to understand how our lives depend upon the courage, the industry, the honesty and integrity of our fellow men; that we may be mindful of their needs, grateful for their faithfulness, and faithful in our responsibilities to them, through Jesus Christ our Lord. *Amen*

103 A LITANY ON THE VOCATION OF THE STUDENT

O most holy God, grant that all our life may be set in such perspective, that we look not mainly to the past nor to the future, nor live only in the experiences of others, but rather know the meaning of our own pilgrimage this day:

That as students we may justify our designation as being those who study, pondering earnestly not only our books and our classwork, but also people about us, the world in its wonder and complexity, the glory and mystery of thy being;

Keep us aware who we are, O Lord.

That we be faithful in carrying out academic assignments, working with a will, not chiefly to impress teachers nor to compete for high standing, but to fulfill our own capacities and our duty to thee;

Keep us aware who we are, O Lord.

That we realize that our likely lot is to become in our lifework what we are today as students, thorough or slipshod, outgoing or selfish, dependable or untrustworthy, setting our own pattern now for the years that are ahead;

Keep us aware who we are, O Lord.

That we let nothing harmful—lack of sleep, overindulgence in food or drink or play, corruption of imagination, or license of behavior—keep us from our principal duty of being faithful to the opportunities thou dost give us as those who study;

Keep us aware who we are, O Lord.

That we see these days on campus not as a vacation from life, irresponsible and unconcerned for our society and its ills, but as a time of opportunity to understand more truly the world in which we live, lay up stock for our journey, and deepen the good in us that it may enlarge the good in all men;

Keep us aware who we are, O Lord.

That we have no false condescension toward those about us, knowing with awe that because we have been given special advantage, much will be expected of us both by society and by thee;

Keep us aware who we are, O Lord.

That we may have our part in this academic community, and in intimate groups within it, but above all that we may have our part in thee and in thy Church, where our true loyalty belongs during these years and in all the years;

> *Keep us aware who we are, O Lord.*

Father of our spirits, who hast opened to each of us a door of opportunity for study, and hast enabled us fittingly to share the life of this intentional fellowship, fulfill within us thy holy purpose, that here we may find the joy and freedom of serving thee and thy kingdom; so may the Lord Christ be continually praised in our midst, and exalted by all our learning and work. *Amen*

104 THREE MEDITATIONS ON LIFE DECISION
[A prayer may well be used as preparation, and the intention is that prayers and resolutions will be prompted by the following Scripture passages and suggestions.]

a. *Ye have not chosen me, but I have chosen you.*
Scripture passage: *Matthew 4:18-22*
Consider that all our powers of mind and body are
> God's gift to us;
> that our thanksgiving is the use of these gifts in his service;
> that these gifts enable us to obey him in a particular way through the career to which he calls us;
> that this calling means for us hardship and adventure, many friends and many enemies.

b. *Beloved of God, called to be saints*
Scripture passage: *Matthew 4:1-11*
Consider that our Lord's temptation was to do the right
> thing in the wrong way;
> that our temptation is often to do the wrong thing;
> that God leads us into the true way and sustains us in following it;
> that he does not guide us against our will;
> that he answers our strivings to know his will for us;

that our strivings begin in being receptive and are
continued in our active obedience to the divine
prompting;

that our security is that peace which the world cannot give;

that our peace is active obedience in the face of
danger and difficulty.

c. *I made myself a servant unto all.*
Scripture passage: *John 13:1-11*
Consider the magnitude of our Lord's service;

that our service begins in realization of our responsibilities and powers;

that in the eyes of God our purpose determines the
importance of our work—not its nature;

that service is the fulfillment of the obligations
which are ours because of our relationships to God
and to men;

that our service to our family, the community and
the nation is interpreted to us by our membership
in the Church;

that the following of a career, under the guidance
of God, is to be our way of expressing our obedience
to him.

Bible passages for further meditations: *Exodus 3:1-14;
Isaiah 6:1-8; Jeremiah 1:4-10; Matthew 3:13-17;
9:35-38; 12:46-50; 19:16-22; 20:17-23; Luke 5:27-28.*

105 A FORM FOR PERSONAL SELF-EXAMINATION

*Thou requirest truth in the inward parts
And shalt make me to understand wisdom secretly.
My soul truly waiteth still upon God
For of him cometh my salvation.*

a. Have I thought out fully enough

the careers open to my choice? . . .

the type of service to God which each would entail
for me? . . .

that work gives meaning to my membership in the Church and in society?

b. Have I always been grateful for

my abilities, my distinctness as a person? . . .
the advice and encouragement of those whom I respect? . . .
the powers which I found were mine through taking my part in common activities? . . .
all the ways God guides me toward finding my work and my place in life?

c. Have I always been ready to admit the anxieties that are caused

by vague unexamined fears? . . .
by financial difficulties? . . .
by family misunderstandings? . . .
by commitments I have already made? . . .
by obligations not of my own making?

d. Am I sometimes inclined

to postpone deliberations about my career because I doubt my abilities and my worth? . . .
to daydream about a possible importance for myself of my own choosing? . . .
to long for safety rather than adventure? . . .
to shrink from consideration of certain careers because of the responsibility and temptations which they appear to have for me? . . .
to forget that a career is a way of serving God and growing in knowledge of him, that this service may be more mature? . . .
to think too briefly about the nature of missionary obligations and how they may concern me? . . .
to ignore the diverse ways in which God reveals his will for me—through events, happenings, friendships, my thinking, and my praying?

e. How can I improve my thinking and my praying so that I may come more fully under the divine guidance?

What practical information do I require to help me to arrive at a decision about my career? . . .
Is the choice about a career to be binding, or in my case can I make a provisional choice?

Lord, what I have not, give me.
Lord, what I know not, teach me.
Lord, what I am not, make me.

Almighty God, whose ways are past wonder, whose desires for us are beyond imagining; grant us wisdom and
daring, that, with thine aid, we may serve thee in all
faithfulness so that we may attain at length thy gracious
promises; through Jesus Christ our Lord. *Amen*

Section Two: Prayers for Purpose in Work

106 FOR THE WORK OF THIS DAY
O Father, light up the small duties of this day.
Help us to believe that glory may dwell in the com-
monest task. *Amen*

We praise thee, O God, that daily work is intended by
thee as a blessing, not a burden nor a drudgery. We
praise thee that the nail driven straight and true, the
furrow well turned, the study honestly engaged, the
chore faithfully fulfilled, the day's business aptly done,
all worship thee in the integrity of tasks worthily completed. Redeem our days by the constant vision that thou
dost accept the praise of our hand and heart in Christ
Jesus our Lord. *Amen*

Gracious God, remember us, we beseech thee, in our
work this day. If it be thy will, give unto us a prosperous
day. May all our work be well done. May we turn nothing out half-done. May we glorify thee by honest good
work; for the sake of him who completed his work for
us, even Jesus Christ. *Amen*

Bless us, O God, with the vision of thy being and beauty,
that in the strength of it we may work without haste and
without sloth, through Christ. *Amen*

Teach us, O gracious Lord, to begin our works with fear,
to go on with obedience, and to finish them in love; and
when we have done our all, to sit humbly down in hope

[106]

and with a cheerful countenance to look up to thee whose promises are faithful and rewards infinite. All this we may do for men, yet they fail us; we may fear and obey, and they forget our service; we may love and hope, yet they neglect our affections: only thou, O Lord, whom we can in no way benefit, dost every way oblige us. *Amen*

107 FOR WORK TO DO
Master,

Give us this day hard work to do,
Work that will tax us and strain us,
Work that will stretch our muscles and engross our minds,
Work that will employ all our powers of body and intellect and heart,
Work, above all, that will further thy cause in the world.

If our work appointed this day be study and training for life,
Reveal unto us our responsibility to thee for the future;
Show us that we are debtors to thyself and to our fellows;
Teach us that every faculty of body and mind must be faithfully prepared,
So that, when our time comes, we may go forth fit instruments for thy service,
Weapons polished and keen, ready suited to thy grasp,
Wherewith thou mayest fight the battles of righteousness and truth,
Vanquishing error, oppression and wrong.

If our work be the teaching and training of others,
Then make our minds pure and humble before thyself,
That no stain of selfishness or lethargy,
Of mean purpose or of low ideals,
May mar this weighty and honorable service
Which thou in thy loving favor hast been pleased to commit to our charge. *Amen*

108 FOR HIGH PURPOSE IN OUR LIFE WORK

Almighty God, send us out into life, not for cheap things, and not for self, but to do battle for thy purposes. We have not been trained for beds of ease. At times we dare to ask that thou wilt lead us to where the struggle is hardest. We ask thee not for easier tasks, but for strength equal to our tasks. We ask not to be left apart with smooth lives dead at heart. Make real to us, O God, the nobility of work, that we may accept its disciplines as the price which leads in the end to the joy of creation, through Christ. *Amen*

O God, enlarge us and make us bold:
against all who cleverly mock at high intentions;
against all who discount any purity in motives;
against all who deny that there is any meaning in life;
against all who guide their lives by expediency;
against all who distort the good news of the gospel;
against all who believe in the power of men apart from thee;
against all who would urge us to look for narrow temporal security;
against all kindly people who would encourage us to lose our souls in exchange for illusory comforts.

We pray, O Lord, for deliverance from all that weakens faith in thee:
from pompous solemnity;
from mistaking earnestness for trust in thee;
from seeking easy answers to large questions;
from being overawed by the self-confident;
from dependence on mood and feelings;
from despondency and loss of self-respect;
from timidity and hesitation in making decisions.
Hear our prayer, O God, for
all who halt, uncertain before alternatives;
all who fear the commonplace;
all who must forego much to achieve little;
all those who are preparing for church vocations;
all others who are also preparing to serve thee according to their several callings.

In Christ we pray. *Amen*

Gracious Lord, we pray for ourselves in this society of the truth, that accepting with gladness the high offices of thought, that seeing clearly, and feeling deeply, we may go forth to be in the world as those who serve; and may thus know that mind of Christ which we would make the manner of our thinking, through Jesus Christ our Lord. *Amen*

Give us, O God, the listening ear and the responsive will. Bring such answer to each sincere and simple prayer as each one of us needs: giving to one of us more courage, and to another self-restraint, and to yet another freedom from selfishness and self-interest. Rescue us from the meager use of thy great gifts. Maintain in us the fidelity of those to whom much has been given, and from whom much will be required; that we may hear at last the kindly benediction, Well done, good and faithful servant: enter into the joy of thy Lord. *Amen*

Our Father in heaven, who hast so made us that we reach attainment only through striving, and who hast placed in our hearts conflicting desires, that we may learn to choose the things that are worthwhile; grant us the grace to choose aright in this and every hour of time, and in every expenditure of strength. Help us to face squarely the responsibilities that go with the moral issues of our time, and to range our personal power and influence on the side of those ideals in which we honestly believe. While we pray and work for peace in the affairs of men, may we never forget that there is no peace in the struggle against evil. Arm us with confidence in the eternal value of all that is true and beautiful and good, and give us strength every hour to do the things we know are right. We ask it in the name of Jesus Christ our Lord. *Amen*

Almighty God, move our hearts as we discern the urgent and difficult issues of our day, that we may be fearless and resourceful in thee:

when machines and systems and governments destroy the meaning of men, help us to revolt against them and change them;

when vast and impersonal industry freezes out the life-blood of human fellowship, help us to discard that pattern for some new one;

when war and preparation for violence become the ground for our whole economy of work and production, show us our tragic folly that we may do away with war and again work for lofty purposes;

when our laziness or desire for luxury means that men and women anywhere must work for less than just wages, curse our ways and bring us to our senses;

when our snobbish class-consciousness drives workers to resentment not for more pay but for recognition as human beings, transform this sorry scheme of relationships, that it may more nearly resemble thy kingdom;

when thy Church, which alone can speak the word of health and healing, coasts along in complacency and smugness, rekindle, O God, her holy commitment to win the world for thee.

So may we as thy children, who have caught glimpses of thy glory even in the mists and confusions of this troubled world, dedicate our lives to achieve that simplicity, equality, and peace which may unite all men as brothers within thy great love, in Christ. *Amen*

109 FOR COURAGE IN OUR VOCATION
O God, when many say that those who start out on their careers cannot follow the life and teachings of their Master, help us find how to preach his Word in shop or office, and to lift others rather than weakly falling to their level. Help us study to improve our social, political, and economic life so as not to be crushed by mere tradition, organization, or entrenched evil. May we never excuse our own follies by saying that under the existing system we could have done no better.

Give us courage to stand for the right when it is unpopular and openly scorned. Show us, above all, how to earn our own honorable living and provide for all the varied needs of life, without sacrificing character and personal integrity. Sustain us while we are trying to work out the details and the application of these general principles for ourselves, and grant that our life in business and profession, as well as our life in church, may lead us to the feet of our Master. *Amen*

Almighty God, the giver of all good things, without whose help all labor is insufficient, and without whose grace all wisdom is folly; grant, we beseech thee, that in this our undertaking, thy Holy Spirit may not be withheld from us, but that we may promote thy glory, and the coming of thy kingdom. Grant this, O Lord, for the sake of Jesus Christ. *Amen*

Our heavenly Father, enable us to be skillful and helpful in our daily tasks; let us not be praised into follies, fattened into materialism, dazzled into sin, mocked into defiance. Help us to live life as thy Son lived it. *Amen*

O God, thou hast set our feet in a large room. We thank thee that among the blessings of this life we can reckon the demands, the opportunities, and the vision of today. We thank thee for the invigorating sense that all things are being made new, and that it is given to us to make traditions as well as to uphold them. We thank thee that thou hast counted us worthy to stand in this day of the coming of the Son of Man. Grant, O Lord, that to live in such glorious times may cleanse us from all pettiness and self-seeking, filling us with a gallant and undaunted spirit, that we may be diffusers of life, strengthening all we meet. *Amen*

Section Three: The Various Occupations

VOCATION IN AGRICULTURE

110 Almighty God, whose Son didst live and work among farming folk, and whose insights have been given liberally in every age to men close to the soil, kindle anew in this generation the holy trust of those who know that a grain of wheat, dying to itself in the earth, bringeth forth fruit. May they glorify thee by loving care over the good earth and all growing things. Deepen in us our discipline to study and obey thy laws of fruitfulness, granting our souls growth in every season by the warm sun and gentle rain of thy Spirit. *Amen*

We thank thee, O God, for our privilege of stewardship over animals and plants; for the wisdom that grows from the experience we inherit; for the speed and economy and the more abundant yield which come with greater technical knowledge and equipment; for thy constant lesson that our control is limited, and that we depend on thee who givest the increase.

So quicken us that by our work we may insist upon the maintenance or renewal of rural communities, on the farm and in the village; that we may achieve a right scale of values in the use of machinery and men; and that we may exult in the marriage of work with worship, with a true sense of the place of agriculture in thine overarching design for all mankind, in Christ. *Amen*

O God, by whose unchanging law the harvest follows the seedtime, and whatsoever is sown is afterward reaped; mercifully grant that we sow not such seed, that they who follow after us reap misery and shame; for Jesus Christ's sake. *Amen*

111 VOCATION IN ARTS AND CRAFTS
Good Lord, we praise thee for all builders, poets, painters, and makers of music, that they may open our blind eyes and unstop our deaf ears to the beauty of thy world. *Amen*

Our Father, who hast so made us that our hearts leap up when they behold loveliness and grace, school our eye and hand and ear that we may trace out after thee the outlines of beauty found about us; that mediating its joy and pleasure among our fellow men, we may thereby publish abroad the gladness which thou hast intended for all thy children, in him who is altogether lovely, Christ Jesus. *Amen*

O thou who art the all-pervading glory of the world, we praise thee for our brothers, the masters of form and color and sound, who have power to unlock for us the vaster spaces of emotion and to lead us by their hand into the reaches of nobler passions. Make them the reverent interpreters of God to man, who see thy face and hear thy voice in all things; that so they may unveil for us the beauties of nature which we have passed unseeing, and the sadness and sweetness of humanity to which our selfishness has made us blind. *Amen*

112   VOCATION IN BUSINESS

Prosper our industries, we pray thee, God most high, that our land may be full with all manner of store, and there be no complaining in our streets; and as thy glorious Son our Lord plied tool and trade on earth, so give to all that labor pride in their work, a just reward, and joy both in supplying need and serving thee; through Jesus Christ our Lord. *Amen*

We pray thee, O God, for those who are pressed by the cares and beset by the temptations of business life. We acknowledge before thee our common guilt for the hardness and deceitfulness of industry and trade which lead all into temptation and cause even the righteous to slip and fall. May thy Spirit, O God, which is ceaselessly pleading within us, prevail at last to bring our business life under Christ's law of service, so that all who share in the processes of factory and trade may grow up into that high consciousness of a divine calling, which blesses those who are the free servants of God and the people. Through Christ our Lord. *Amen*

O God, thou alone knowest the problems we meet and the obstacles before us as we start our careers, trying to deserve respect and confidence. Show us what is good and right and true in our day, to make thy way plain to us

[113]

in our noisy, busy, highly organized, and complicated world. Make our religion real and vital, that it may daily give us assurance and power and hope; and grant that in our chosen field we too may be preachers of thy Word, through Jesus Christ our Lord. *Amen*

113 VOCATION IN THE CHURCH

Guard those, O God, who look toward the ministry of thy Church, in parish, classroom, mission, or any other place; keep them from pride or false piety, empowering them neither to shrink from the world nor to embrace it without restraint; teach them deeply by thy Spirit and thy Word, that they may store up by study and secret prayer both truth and radiance for the days of their task ahead; and thus by serving thee, serve others in Christ's name. *Amen*

Good Lord, we pray for all who would lead man's long thoughts beyond the things that are known into the world which is unknown, that their faith may prepare for us a place in the infinite mystery. Bless all who unselfishly bring their knowledge to the service of the world, that they may prove their learning by their works, and give that vision without which the people perish. In Christ. *Amen*

Ever-gracious God, bless the many ministers of religion of every creed, in every land. Take from them all prejudice, all love of priestly power, all fear of men. Make them true witnesses to the gospel of Christ, humble, faithful, and unafraid. *Amen*

Almighty God, who hast set in thy Church some with gifts to teach and help and administer, in diversity of operation but of the same Spirit; grant to all such, we beseech thee, grace to wait on the ministry which they have received with simplicity, diligence, and cheerfulness; that none think of himself more highly than he ought to think, and none seek another man's calling, but rather to be found faithful over a few things, and to receive praise of Christ in his own work. *Amen*

114 VOCATION IN COUNSELING AND PERSONNEL

O Lord, to whose blessed Son all men took their problems and difficulties, raise up amongst us men and women trained and humble to guide the choices and lives of those about them. We know, O God, what perplexities and confusions surround us all, and beg thy forgiveness for anything we have added to the frustrations of our friends and loved ones. Make us affirmative and strong to heal, sensitive to inner tragedy, skilled to recognize the sources of difficulty, constant in our hope for every child of thy love. So may we avoid our Lord's condemnation of blind guides for the blind, but rather lead others to light because we see thee clearly, the Light of the world. *Amen*

We thank thee, O God, for deeper understanding of the mind and instincts of man, for the shattering of our pride, and for the humility which comes from perceiving our share in the deep instinctive forces of all creation; for the healing of the lunatic and possessed, for the dispersal of neurosis and obsession.

Grant, O merciful Father, that we may ever remember those committed to our care, not as cases but as persons, never using our knowledge as power, but with self-effacement and love. We pray for non-Christian counselors and advisers, that thou mayest use their skill in spite of their convictions; and for ourselves that our faith may commend thee to them as the author of all health and wholeness. *Amen*

115 VOCATION IN EDUCATION

Grant, O Lord, to all who prepare for teaching or leadership in schools, that they may be bold enough always to say what they think, and alert enough always to think what they say, in him who taught as one having authority, even Christ. *Amen*

O God, we pray thee for all who prepare for teaching, that they may have eyes to see the greatness of their vocation. . .

For those who have no love for youth nor for teaching, grant courage that they may cut the bonds which tie them to the profession, or if that cannot be, courage to believe that Christ can give them that change of temperament which they need. . .

For those who have just left their training, and in their teaching tasks are faced with lack of sympathy for high ideals, or are disheartened by conditions under which they work, give courage, O Lord, that they may keep their vision, and perseverance to work it out in more living ways. . .

For those who in teaching find it hard to keep the eternal youth and freshness which children and youth demand, that they may find in Christ a continual renewal and deepening of personality. In Christ. *Amen*

O God, grant to all those who teach an abiding consciousness that they are co-workers with thee, thou great Teacher of humanity. We bless thee for the free and noble spirit which breathes with quickening power upon the life of learning in our day: give us men and women of large mind and loving heart, that they may make that spirit our common possession by their teaching and example, through Christ. *Amen*

116 VOCATION IN ENGINEERING AND TECHNICAL WORK

Almighty God, who dost claim the beginning and the end of our work, grant to this generation of engineers and technicians such wisdom that they may glorify thee, both as they begin their career dealing with things, and end it dealing with people. Thou hast given us new dazzling power for good or ill over all the world: may we never measure men by slide rule or test tube, nor avoid our responsibility to society by appeals to imagined progress or mere gain of nation or commerce. Keep us humble explorers sent out by a restlessness thou hast placed in our hearts;

inventors finding what thou hast already known in all eternity;

proclaimers of new truth because millions have labored in thee through all the years to bring us to this hour of discovery.

So may we be a blessing and not a bane to thy people everywhere on the earth, in Christ. *Amen*

O thou Creator and Redeemer of man, whom thou willest to have dominion over the earth, and to have communion with thee, we praise thee and give thee glory.

Forgive us as we imagine that we are lords of truth, treating knowledge as a source of power to be grasped at for our own ends.

Forgive us as we lightly accept all created things, forgetting that through all the ages thou hast worked to bring the universe to this hour that we might know it.

Forgive us as we lack reverence for life, denying our stewardship over living things.

Forgive us as we attempt to fit persons into a scheme of thought derived from our knowledge of things.

Forgive us as we become lost amid the detail and techniques of our work.

Forgive us as we labor to the danger rather than to the benefit of man.

In all things, O God, as Christ our Lord was made perfect through obedience and suffering, may we through acceptance of monotony and routine bring forth order and well-being to man, in him. *Amen*

Broaden, O Father, the training of engineers and all who deal with inanimate materials and principles in their work, that they may discover and cherish the treasures of human experience in art and history and philosophy, and thus may be prepared not only to make their living, but as well to live. We pray in Christ. *Amen*

117 VOCATION IN THE HOME

Lord of all life, deepen in us all the sense of our calling within our families. By thy grace, may we not take parenthood lightly, nor enter into its joy without prayer and humility. With insight born of thee, may we take with becoming seriousness our responsibility to our own parents and other kinsfolk, knowing that our love for them shows forth our love for thee. Redeem us from arrogance and solitariness, and by all our studying and learning, show us how to live in concord with this generation and the next, through Christ. *Amen*

O God, may our lives be crowned with a great love for someone who will help us to serve thee and to use our lives for the highest purposes. Help us to find real love and to solve under thy guidance all the problems that go with choice of a life partner, and with the establishment of a home which thou wouldst bless, through Jesus Christ our Lord. *Amen*

Almighty God, who knowest our nobility and our shame, deliver us from any relationship which we must one day conceal from our helpmeet and from our children, that keeping ourselves in clean readiness for their affection and trust, we may be strong to refuse evil and choose good, through Christ. *Amen*

Eternal God, whose Son knew brotherhood and fatherhood from his own home and hearthside, prepare us during these years for life within the circle of a family of our own. Enable us to lay hold on those gifts of maturity, patience, sharing, love, and humor which grace a household and knit loved ones together. Endue us with wisdom to share life partnership, to train the young, to take part in neighborly friendship, and to unite our family with the whole family of faith. So do thou equip us for the awesome and joyful tasks of home, that we may be equal to the claims to be made upon us by affection and dependence, and by our kinship with others and with thee. *Amen*

118

O Ruler of men, forbid that any should study law mainly to exert power over their fellow men, mainly to outwit their opponents, or mainly to benefit by large fees: give lawyers and judges and all who have civil power over their fellows, that due nobility of purpose which relates them to the whole realm of justice and truth as these are known in thee, who art all righteousness and honor. *Amen*

O God, who art the author and giver of law, from whom alone all just designs and righteous judgments proceed, give unto all those who frame, interpret, or administer human law the counsel of thy Holy Spirit, that they may know themselves thy ministers. Suffer them neither to be swayed by the prejudices nor to appeal to the weaknesses of others; but to deal fairly, counsel wisely, and quit themselves manfully in all matters; to be the servants of all men but the hirelings of none, and so to hasten the coming of the kingdom of God on earth, for which we pray. *Amen*

Thou Giver of wisdom, enable us to attain such knowledge as may qualify us to direct the doubtful and instruct the ignorant, to prevent wrongs and terminate contentions, for Jesus Christ's sake. *Amen*

O God, thou great governor of all the world, we pray thee to strengthen the sense of duty in our political life. Grant that the servants of the state may feel ever more deeply that any diversion of their public powers for private ends is a betrayal of their country. Bring to an end the stale days of party cunning. Give our leaders a new vision of the possible future of our country, and set their hearts on fire with large resolves. Raise up a new generation of men and women in government, who will have the faith and daring of the kingdom of God in their hearts, and who will enlist for life in a holy warfare for the freedom and rights of the people. *Amen*

119 O Eternal One, who didst fashion the universe with thy hands, keep us aware of the rugged power of common work faithfully done. Save us from the blasphemy of dealing with human workers as though they were parts of a machine, or mere numbers, or commodities to be bought and sold. Grant to all who lead these laboring men and women keenness of vision, breadth of spirit, and concern for the good of all, that their followers may receive a just share of the fruits of their toil, and lasting satisfaction in the process of work itself. Hasten the day, O God, when partisanship may give way to partnership, uniting those who direct by the power of their minds with those who labor by the strength and skill of their hands. Thus may we glorify the master Workman of the race, even Christ our Lord. *Amen*

O God, we pray thee for the industrial workers of the nation. When they strive for leisure and health and a better wage, do thou grant their cause success, but teach them not to waste their gain in fleeting passions, but to use it in building fairer homes and a nobler manhood. So may we see among our brothers a great body of workers, strong of limb, clear of mind, fair in temper, glad to labor, conscious of their worth, and striving together for the final brotherhood of all men. Through Christ. *Amen*

O Father, help thou the labor movement of our day to be worthy of its heritage. Unite in high purpose the workers in the factory and on the farm. Preserve them from temptation to selfish complacency in partial gains for any favored craft or race or nation. Guard their leaders from lust for personal power. Guide them in the service of the common good, that the workers of all lands may stand shoulder to shoulder for justice and peace among the nations. *Amen*

Our heavenly Father, as we newly discern in our time the blessedness of work with our hands, to give clarity to the distraught mind and serenity to the clouded spirit, give us grace both to undertake manual work ourselves, and to make it meaningful for others. Whatever we can do to make significant every job, whatever justice can make all toilers free from resentfulness and vexation, inspire us by our lifework to find these answers. Thus may we give ourselves to achieving true freedom for all whose task has been drudgery or routine without hope. We pray in Christ. *Amen*

120 VOCATION IN MEDICINE, NURSING, AND DENTISTRY

O Lord, make all who aspire to heal human ills co-operators with thee in thine eternal work of bringing order and love to bear everywhere. As we seek health for the bodies of others, keep us mindful that our true health is to be members of the Body of Christ. As we seek wholeness for their minds, may there be in us that mind which was also in Christ Jesus. So in all ways may we know that we are instruments of thy concern, our skill thy gift, our knowledge thine endowment, our care and carefulness a showing forth of his love who came that we may have life. *Amen*

O merciful Father, who hast made man's body to be a temple of thy Holy Spirit, sanctify, we pray thee, all those whom thou hast called to the study and practice of the arts of healing, as to the prevention of disease and pain. Bless their work, that they may be followers of the Good Physician Christ, and give comfort to those whom he lived and died to save. *Amen*

O God of all things whole, keep aloft before all in medical careers such idealism as shall redeem them from pettiness and undue ambition, freeing them into the joy of ready service. Guard them against losing sight of far-off goals during their years of study. As they enter into practice, deliver them from possessiveness within their profession. Spare them as they deal with any patient from the pretensions of omniscience and from dignified ignorance, and as they deal with any colleague, from pride and competitiveness. Enhance in them the age-old devotion and integrity of those who know their life task to be a holy calling under thee, healing and comforting and bringing gladness among their fellow men in Christ's name. *Amen*

We praise thee, O God, for doctors and nurses: for their gentleness and patience, for their knowledge and skill. Make them apostles of thy kingdom, which is the reign of cleanliness and self-restraint and the dominion of health and joyous life. May they never through the pressure of need or ambition surrender the sense of a divine mission, and become hirelings who serve only for money. Though they deal with the frail body of man, may they have an abiding sense of the eternal value of the life residing in it; that by the call of faith and hope, they may summon to their aid the mysterious spirit of man and the powers of thy all-pervading life. Through Christ, the healer of our spirits. *Amen*

121 VOCATION IN MILITARY LIFE

O Lord of hosts, guide thou those whose life task lies ahead in the military forces of this land. As their goal is not violence but order, not the chaos of war but discipline, keep their minds clear and their intentions high. May their obedience be a token of their absolute allegiance to thee; their readiness for action a token of courage in spiritual conflict, their comradeship in arms a token of Christian community and sharing. Through their loyalty and service, bring ever closer the day when no nation shall boast its military might, but all nations act as one to put down injustice in the earth, by the power of Jesus Christ. *Amen*

Grant, O Lord, that our soldiers may be brave in battle, highhearted in hardship, dauntless in defeat and gentle in victory. Be with all those who have trained themselves in times of peace to serve their country in the day of war; give them endurance and self-control, skill and courage, in the duty now before them. *Amen*

Defend, O God, all who with plane or ship or bomb or gun seek to protect what they hold dear, that they may not give way to arrogance among their fellows or before their enemy, nor put their hope in violence as the greatest power known to men. Guard them against boredom in routine, against frustration over the chain of command, against license in their moral living, and against cynicism about the government they serve. May they find time for prayer and friendliness, nor allow any barrier of rank or achievement to cut them off from all their military companions. So may they glorify thee in their work and worship, through Christ. *Amen*

We pray thee, O Lord, to raise up men and women in the armed forces who will keep their perspective as Christians, serving conscience as they serve their commanders. Forgive us for our part in the selfishness and fear which beckon the gaunt specter of war among the nations, and may our penitence bring us soon to establish peace under law for all peoples. *Amen*

122 VOCATION IN SCIENTIFIC RESEARCH

Good Lord, bless those who seek for new truth, that believing more light is yet to break, they may be sustained in their searching by faith that thou art, and that thou art the rewarder of them that diligently seek thee. We pray that all scientists, looking upon the face of nature, may see order in its variety and law in its constancy, and may teach men to live upon earth in confidence and without fear. Through Christ. *Amen*

Almighty God, we praise thee for the courage of lonely explorers into the realms of fact, and for the sharing with fellowship which advances all scientific discovery. Save those whose life is spent in research from irresponsibility for the end products of their work, sensitive to the whole meaning of what they do. Forbid, Lord, that our cleverness should thrust us toward disaster, or our earnest experiments deliver mankind to unforeseen tragedy. Seeing our work as our vocation in thee, may we make it serve the vast intention of thy love in redeeming the world, and in binding all truth together in him in whom all things consist, Christ Jesus our Lord. *Amen*

Lord, we pray for humility in our learning, and frankness to acknowledge that ours is but one of many avenues of truth, not the only one nor yet the most important; and for grace to remember that knowledge does not itself make perfect. Grant us watchfulness that we become not slaves to our techniques, methods, or machines. Particularly do we pray that the isolation of research may never blind us to life as unified in Christ our Lord. *Amen*

123 VOCATION IN SOCIAL WORK
Almighty God, the earthly work of whose Son was among the crowds, and in households, and with the solitary questioner, grant thy guidance to all who look to social work as their life task. As their profession has come forth out of the Church, born of Christian concern for all who are in need, show them constantly the ground and goal of their work as redemption of mankind in the pattern of thy love. When new resources expand their programs, guard them from lapsing into impersonality and case-mindedness, inwardly cynical or stoical about life, unaware of thy glory. So may all who love their fellow men work and pray together for thy blessed kingdom. *Amen*

O thou, who hast perfectly revealed the will of God and the true nature of man, we pray for the men and women who are giving their lives to improve the lot of their comrades, but who have yet been turned from thee by the poverty of our discipleship. Forgive us, and help us to learn thy will from them; and grant them to realize the eternal value of thy word and life, in Christ. *Amen*

O God, who hast made us members one of another in the family of mankind, and hast submitted us to the laws of mutual dependence, grant that in our study of social forces we may not lose our sympathy, and that in the meeting of person with person we may see thy Son as in our midst. Bless us with gifts of accuracy, thoroughness, impartiality, gratitude to tradition, and a responsible awareness of future generations, that all our study and work may exalt thy name among men and place thy love at the center of all human relationships, in Christ. *Amen*

124 VOCATION IN WRITING AND JOURNALISM
Deliver us, O Lord, from having skill to write, with nothing to write about; from caring for smooth expression more than for rugged truth; from having ready words upon our lips but a sparse vocabulary of the soul. Show us that great communication comes from great conviction. Deepen our everyday life so that our opinions, our impressions, our sharing of the excitement of life, may all be prompted by our joy in knowing thee and witnessing to thy manifold wonder and beauty, in Christ our Lord. *Amen*

O thou great Source of truth and knowledge, we remember before thee all those whose calling it is to gather and winnow the facts for informing the people. Since the sanity and wisdom of a nation are in their charge, may they count it shame to set the baser passions of men on fire for the sake of gain. May they never suffer themselves to be used in drugging the mind of the people with falsehood and prejudice. Put into their hands the shining sword of truth, and make them worthy successors of the great champions of the people who held truth to be a holy thing. *Amen*

We thank thee, O God, for thy gifts of poets and writers, for those who have scorned delights and lived laborious days, in poverty and isolation, at the call of letters. We praise thee for all excellence of impression and all communication of insight, for all challenge to frivolity and all deepening of wisdom through writing and reading. Grant to writers and journalists in this generation a sense of their vocation, skilled craftsmanship in words, careful scholarship, and sound judgment. May they rejoice in a new understanding of thy creation and redemption in all they read and write, guided in its use that it may be to thy glory. So may the beauty of words be seen as the beauty of holiness, through him who came amongst us as the living Word. *Amen*

Section Four: For Others in the World of Work

125 FOR THE UNEMPLOYED

O God, thou Lord of the vineyard, who wouldst not that any should stand idle in the marketplace, hear our prayer for the multitudes without employment or assurance of livelihood; and in the largeness of thy loving wisdom, declare unto us the counsels to help and heal all our distresses; through Jesus Christ our Lord. *Amen*

Lord God, have mercy upon us for our ignorance and greed which have brought to multitudes starvation in the midst of plenty.
From sense of our own virtue at some slight charity to the unemployed,
    Good Lord, deliver us.
From luxury and display, while many have not where to lay their heads,
    Good Lord, deliver us.
From heedless comfort in the security of our homes, while families of the poor are evicted from their homes, their children and furniture upon the street,
    Good Lord, deliver us.
From methods of private or public relief which save the bodies of men but destroy their inmost spirit; from hurting the finer sensibilities of men and women, robbing them of their pride and self-respect,
    Good Lord, deliver us.
From false notions that by preaching we can save the souls of men, while unemployment breaks their hearts, unbalances their minds, destroys their homes, tempts

them beyond measure, visits want and disease upon their children, turns the heart to bitterness, hatred, and rebellion, or to hopelessness, despair, and death,

Good Lord, deliver us.

From ever forgetting the forlorn figure of the unemployed; from failure to see that our social fabric is as shabby as his coat,

Good Lord, deliver us.

From satisfaction with any revival of trade or renewed prosperity while multitudes still can find no work,

Good Lord, deliver us.

That our conscience may know no rest until unemployment is abolished,

We beseech thee, good Lord.

That it may please thee to guide us quickly into the good life in which there shall be peace and plenty; a sharing of labor and leisure and joy by all the children of men,

We beseech thee, good Lord. Amen

126 FOR THOSE IN THE WRONG VOCATION

Almighty God, whose way is sometimes hid from us even when we earnestly seek it, we pray for those who in their preparation or in their work now realize that they are in the wrong field. Grant them courage and adaptability, O Lord, to shift even now to the vocation wherein they hear thy call clearly; or, if that way be closed, give them a new vision of their present task, that it may be changed, or they be changed, to serve acceptably where they are.

Guard us against all restlessness and lack of trust, against discouragement over small reverses, against overreaching our abilities or underestimating the power thou canst give us to endure and to conquer. So may our tranquillity be grounded in thee, and all our choices be governed by thy holy will, through Christ our Lord. *Amen*

127 FOR WORKERS OF TIMES PAST

O gracious God, we thank thee for all those who have gone before us, showing us the glory of vocation in thee:

For the testimony of the saints in all ages;

For those who in times of darkness kept the lamp of faith burning;

For great souls who saw visions of larger truth and dared to declare it;

For all who fought for truth and liberty;

For the multitude of quiet and gracious souls whose presence has purified and sanctified the world;

For preachers and evangelists raised up to declare the message of God with power;

For all faithful witnesses to the life that is in Christ;

For all true and acceptable service rendered unto thee, O blessed God, we give thee thanks and praise this day. *Amen*

Our heavenly Father, show us how to encourage those who have labored long and well for good causes, and now await the sunset and the call to thee. Help us to support those in middle life who are becoming discouraged and wearied with many burdens and many problems. May they feel that we have been worth working for, and that we embody some of their dearest hopes and ideals. Bless all those everywhere who work in thy name and show the spirit of thy Son, in whom we pray. *Amen*

The Church

Section One: Its Life and Ministry

128 A LITANY ON THE WORK AND WORSHIP OF THE CHURCH

Almighty God, we praise and glorify thy holy name for thy Church, the pillar and ground of the truth, the mother of saints in all ages and all lands:

For the great cloud of witnesses with which we are encompassed, the noble army of martyrs, the goodly company of the prophets, and all men holy and humble of heart,

We praise and glorify thy holy name.

For the goodly heritage thou hast given us, for all opportunities of work and worship in thy Church, for the sacraments and all means of grace, by which our bodies are made temples of thy Spirit and our minds instruments of thy truth,

We praise and glorify thy holy name.

That thou hast in our day kindled in our hearts a longing for the unity of thy Church and a hope of its accomplishment,

We praise and glorify thy holy name.

From all slighting of thy love and neglect of thy benefits offered us freely in Christ Jesus,

Deliver us, good Lord.

From halfhearted following of our Master, and want of power and conviction in our preaching,

Deliver us, good Lord.

From all coldness and indifference toward the missionary work of thy Church; and from lack of sympathy and prayer for those without the gospel of Christ,

Deliver us, good Lord.

From sentimentality and insincerity in worship, from lack of zeal for truth, and from trifling with our own souls or those of others,

Deliver us, good Lord.

[129]

That amid the change and unrest of the present time, the Church may be cleansed and renewed by thy Spirit,
Keep us true to thee, O God.
That the Church may take its full share in all efforts for social reform, for the healing of the sick, the clothing of the naked, the feeding of the hungry,
Keep us true to thee, O God.
That the Church may be freed from prejudice and fear in its attitude toward the problems of race, of economic justice, and of the equal place of women in our society,
Keep us true to thee, O God.
That the Church may be zealous in laboring for the removal of oppression and injustice and the promotion of righteousness and peace,
Keep us true to thee, O God.
That the Church may take its place in all national movements, so that the Name which is above every name may be known and magnified throughout the earth,
Keep us true to thee, O God.
That those who lead the thought and action of thy Church may be given hearts and minds open to thy guidance,
Keep us true to thee, O God.
Gracious Father, we humbly beseech thee for thy holy catholic Church. Fill it with all truth, in all truth with all peace. Where it is corrupt, purge it; where it is in error, direct it; where it is superstitious, rectify it; where anything is amiss, reform it; where it is right, strengthen and confirm it; where it is in want, furnish it; where it is divided and rent asunder, make up the breaches of it, O thou holy One of Israel, for the sake of Jesus Christ our Lord and Savior. *Amen*

129 A LITANY FOR A NEW VISION OF THE CHURCH

O God of grace, we pray thee that our Church may become alive again with the fire of her first charity, fearless of danger and reckless unto death, in the splendor of that Life which is the light of the world:

That our Church may be worthy of her new-found liberty, persistent in reform, active in benevolence, trusting the people, and ever faithful to the Jerusalem which is above and is free and the mother of us all,

Grant now thy grace, O God.

That our American people, so adventurous and so strong, may in each generation rise up to claim their heritage and make the Church their own,

Grant now thy grace, O God.

That our young men and women may have sight of her, pure and fair as a bride adorned, coming down from God out of heaven,

Grant now thy grace, O God.

That our eyes may kindle to her beauty, when she looks forth as the morning, fair as the moon, clear as the sun, and mighty as an army with banners,

Grant now thy grace, O God.

That her old men may dream dreams, and her young men see visions; that her sons and her daughters may prophesy, bearing eager witness of her beauty to the world,

Grant now thy grace, O God.

That all her members, putting self aside, disinterested and pure in heart, may seek the truth, and see God, and rejoice in his truth,

Grant now thy grace, O God.

That her ministers may be good and wise, strong and very courageous, competent in their work, and faithful in their witness,

Grant now thy grace, O God.

That her councils and conventions may be keen to go forward, filled with the wisdom of the Spirit, to rebuild the walls of Jerusalem,

Grant now thy grace, O God.

That all the people of the city of God may take up their citizenship, and be fellow workers in the democracy of Christ,

Grant now thy grace, O God.

That her scholars may have disciples, her prophets hearers, her saints imitators, and all her pioneers many multitudes to follow in their steps,

Grant now thy grace, O God.

That we may forsake that love of party which keeps us from loving one another; and so, coming in friendship together, we and all our brothers in Christ may find the overpowering love of God, which shall knit us together in one united Church,

Grant now thy grace, O God.

And, finally, that the Church, with love recovered in her midst, may teach all men to love one another, and all nations to dwell together in helpfulness and friendship, reconciled and redeemed,

Grant now thy grace, O God, and bless us now and for evermore. Amen

130 O God, we pray for thy Church, which is set today amid the perplexities of a changing order, and face to face with a great new task. We remember with love the nurture she gave to our spiritual life in its infancy, the tasks she set for our growing strength, the influence of the devoted hearts she gathers, the steadfast power for good she has exerted. When we compare her with all other human institutions, we rejoice, for there is none like her.

But when we judge her by the mind of her Master, we bow in pity and contrition. O baptize her afresh with the life-giving spirit of Jesus! Grant her a new birth, though it be with the travail of repentance and humiliation. Bid her cease from seeking her own life, lest she lose it. Make her valiant to give up her life to humanity, that like her crucified Lord she may mount by the path of the cross to a higher glory. Through him whose living Body is thy Church. *Amen*

131 Lord, revive thy Church, beginning with me. *Amen*

132 O Lord of changeless power and endless life, be favorable unto thy Church throughout the world. Gather, enlighten, sanctify, and sustain it by thy Holy Spirit. Give us more and more to trust the silent working of thy perpetual grace, which bringeth forth in Christ the salvation of men. And let the whole world know that the things which were cast down are being raised up, and the things which had grown old are being made new, and all things are returning to the perfection of him from whom they came. *Amen*

133 Remember, O Lord, thy Church; redeem her from all evil, and perfect her in thy love. Strengthen and preserve her by the Word and sacraments. Enlarge her borders, that so thy gospel may be preached to all nations, and gather men from all the ends of the earth into the kingdom which thou hast prepared. *Amen*

134 O God, to whom the generations have lifted their hands and hearts in prayer since man became man, we would take our place in that great succession of souls whose chief joy in life has been the knowledge of thee. Make us cleaner, stronger, truer, because we have sat at the feet of the wise and noble and the saintly of the ages. May we be stronger comrades in thine eternal work, as we find it revealed in the matchless life of thy Son, our Master, Jesus Christ. *Amen*

135 We beseech thee, O Lord, to guide thy Church with thy perpetual governance that it may walk warily in times of quiet, and boldly in times of trouble, through Jesus Christ our Lord. *Amen*

136 O Lord, be with all that labor and suffer for
the freedom of thy gospel and the purity of thy Word.
Defend them from the world's cold, and the Church's
hate; from error, and haste, and passionate sin; from
sloth, and pride, and the fear of man. *Amen*

137 Spirit of the living God, Source of light and
life, who in the days of old, when men were wandering
in the mist of their own thoughts, spake to them through
prophets and guided them by apostles into the way of
righteousness and truth: we beseech thee to raise up in
these difficult days an increasing number of wise and
faithful men and women, filled with prophetic fire and
apostolic zeal, by whose ministry the Church may be
quickened and thy kingdom greatly advanced. *Amen*

138 We love thy courts, O Christ, and entreat thee
to send light and peace into thy sanctuary. Cleanse thy
temple with the fire of thy Word and the baptism of thy
blood. Make the place of thy crucified feet glorious. Arm
thy prophets with the sword of thy spirit, and thy ministers with the word of reconciliation; and bring all thy
servants to the obedience of faith and the kingdom of
heaven. *Amen*

Section Two: Its Unity

139 Almighty God, in whom is calmness, peace,
and concord; heal thou the divisions which separate thy
children from one another, and enable them to keep the

unity of the Spirit in the bond of peace. While there are
diversities of knowledge and of faith, and we cannot all
be of the same mind, may we be made one in brotherly
love, and in devotion to thy holy will. *Amen*

140 Lord, thou whose Son didst pray
That all thy children might be one in thee,
We come with repentance for the sin of useless division,
And for the secret vice of pride.
We beg forgiveness for harsh judgment,
For prejudice nourished as a virtue,
For self-will,
For scorn of others,
Whose experience before thee is as valid as our own.
We look with consternation upon the broken fabric of
        thy Church,
Split by schism,
More anxious to save a fragment than the whole of man-
        kind.
For all mean attitudes,
For all denial of the worth of other views,
For all exclusiveness which has kept out men of good-
        will,
Receive our contrition
And heal us of the sin which keeps us apart.
Teach us what it means
To "keep the unity of the Spirit in the bond of peace."
Open our eyes to the insight of others,
Help us to appreciate those of other lands
And of other races
Who differing from us in much
Are yet one with us in faith.
Let no little matter obscure the blinding fact of Christ;
No small opinion hide from us his power to redeem the
        world.
For problems beyond our minds to solve, grant us pa-
        tience;
For tasks too great for our weak hands, give us faith;

For all tedious steps in discovering the way,
Endow us with necessary grace;
So that ends we cannot see, our children's children shall
    accomplish.
Through Jesus Christ our Lord. *Amen*

141 O God, our heavenly Father, thou hast loved
and cared for all the generations of the past, as they
struggled toward a better understanding of thee. In our
own modern day of freedom, make us so free that we
shall want to do thy will and avoid the errors of the past.
Where there are churches to be united, may they first
find thee and keep close to thee forever. May we have a
part in this great enterprise, bringing a new spirit of
unity and progressiveness to all the churches. Give us
religion that is ever going ahead, ever shaping its discipleship with Jesus in new and better forms. *Amen*

142 O Lord, how long
   Shall we say we are all brethren,
   That we love our Father in heaven,
      And our life give it the lie?

O Lord, how long
   Shall we speak of love,
   Of our hearts going out to mankind,
      And our love be asleep?

O Lord, how long
   Shall we talk of prayer,
   And rejoice in the beauty of worship,
      And our prayer be a dream?

O Lord, how long
    Shall we bow down to Christ,
    Call him Lord, preach his Word,
      And he know us not?

O Lord, how long
    Is the light of truth flashing,
    The Son of Man coming,
    To be rejected, too, of this generation?
O Lord, how long?

143 O God, the Father of our Lord Jesus Christ, our only Savior, the Prince of peace, give us grace seriously to lay to heart the great dangers we are in by our divisions. Take away all hatred and prejudice, and whatsoever else may hinder us from godly union and concord, through Jesus Christ our Lord. *Amen*

144 A LITANY FOR THE VARIOUS COMMUNIONS
    Let us give thanks for the gifts and graces of each great division of Christendom:
For the ROMAN CATHOLIC CHURCH: its glorious traditions, its disciplines in holiness, its worship, rich with the religious passion of the centuries; its noble company of martyrs, doctors, and saints;
    We thank thee, O Lord, and bless thy holy name.
For the EASTERN ORTHODOX CHURCH: its secret treasure of mystic experience; its marvelous liturgy; its regard for the collective life and its common will as a source of authority;
    We thank thee, O Lord, and bless thy holy name.
For the great Protestant and evangelical communions:
For the CONGREGATIONALIST concern for the rightful independence of the soul and of the group;

We thank thee, O Lord, and bless thy holy name.
For the BAPTIST churches, stressing personal regeneration and the conscious relation of the mature soul to its Lord;

We thank thee, O Lord, and bless thy holy name.
For power among METHODISTS to awaken the conscience of Christians to our social evils; and for their emphasis upon the witness of experience and the fruits of the disciplined life;

We thank thee, O Lord, and bless thy holy name.
For the PRESBYTERIAN reverence for the sovereignty of God and their confidence in his faithfulness to his covenant; for their sense of the moral law, expressing itself in constitutional government;

We thank thee, O Lord, and bless thy holy name.
For the witness to the perpetual real presence of the inner light in every human soul borne by the Religious SOCIETY OF FRIENDS and for their faithful continuance of a free prophetic ministry and Christian nonviolence;

We thank thee, O Lord, and bless thy holy name.
For the LUTHERAN CHURCH; its devotion to the grace of God and the Word of God, enshrined in the ministry of the Word and sacraments;

We thank thee, O Lord, and bless thy holy name.
For the ANGLICAN CHURCH; its reverent and temperate ways, through its Catholic heritage and its Protestant conscience; its yearning over the divisions of Christendom, and its longing to be used as a house of reconciliation;

We thank thee, O Lord, and bless thy holy name.
For the numberless FREE CHURCHES, many humble and without comeliness, in slum and country place and town, speaking the gospel to those unwelcome or uninspired in other congregations;

We thank thee, O Lord, and bless thy holy name.
O God, grant unto all these families within thy great Church, that as they come from the East and from the West to sit down in thy kingdom, each may lay at thy feet that special grace and excellence with which thou in times past hast endowed it, in Christ. *Amen*

145 We thank thee, O Lord, for all Councils of Churches, and for the hope and foretaste of the unity of thy people which they afford. Grant thy blessing upon all efforts of the Councils toward sharing of Christian thought and action; guide their leaders, and to all their member Churches give the spirit of fellowship and the will to find a way to the healing of all our divisions; that so at last we may all be truly one in thee, and glorify thee in all the world. *Amen*

Section Three: Its World Mission

146 O God, thou hast made thyself known to us in Jesus Christ, and to other races thou hast made thyself known in the lives of holy and inspired men. We believe, O Lord, that in the life and teaching of Jesus is the consummation of all truth, that thou dost mean this truth to be for all mankind, and that we are called to share it with them.

But how shall we convey to others that of which we have understood so little, that which in some ways they have understood so much better than ourselves? Give us, we pray thee, such clear knowledge of the truth as it is in Jesus, that we may recognize it wherever we find it, and such sure hold of it that others may see it in us. *Amen*

147 A MEDITATION ON "GO YE THEREFORE"
Jesus came and spake unto them saying, All power is given unto me in heaven and in earth.
It is our mission
To believe that Jesus Christ is Lord and Savior, that in his face we have seen the light of the knowledge of the glory of God:

[139]

That we may know that God is judge and king, ruler over nature, disposer of kingdoms, in whose hand lie the destinies of nations;

That we may know that God is merciful and good, full of compassion and tender care; whose love is spontaneous, free; whose goodness is everlasting;

That we may know that God so loved the world that he gave his only-begotten Son, not to condemn the world, but to free it from the bondage of sin and death.

Go ye therefore
It is our mission
To be separated unto the gospel:

That we may be heralds of a message distinguishable from our culture, our social mores, our secular standards;

That we may be witnesses not of any race, any class, any denomination, any nation;

That we may be witnesses both in Jerusalem and in all Judaea and unto the uttermost parts of the world, there, to make known to all the Lord Jesus Christ as their divine Savior;

That we may be uneasy and troubled when we are faithless to witness in our work whatever and wherever it may be.

Go ye therefore and teach all nations
It is our mission
To reach every man, woman, and child, to give light unto them that sit in darkness, that every knee may bend before him.

That non-Christians in our community, on our street, in our clubs, under our flag may hear;

That the Hindu and Moslem may believe;

That the Communist may confess the name of Jesus Christ;

That all without him now may know him.

Go . . . baptizing them in the name of the Father, and of the Son, and of the Holy Spirit
It is our mission
To be ourselves new creatures in Christ,

That as we go to others we may grow in grace and knowledge, purer vessels to reveal the holiness of God.

To lead others into discipleship:
That the old within, slander, envy, strife, may pass away
and the new, kindness, meekness, longsuffering, may
overflow.
To include all disciples in a fellowship whose head is
Christ:
That this fellowship, the Church, may be one in Him,
sharing together his life that was given for the sins of
the world;
That this fellowship may be holy, consecrated, disciplined, faithful to its mission to preach and make disciples of all nations;
That this fellowship may be universal, embracing all
types of men—the learned, the ignorant, the high, the
low, the white, the black, the brown, the yellow, that
they may be one flock with one shepherd;
That this fellowship may be eternal, an endless line of
splendor reaching back to its Lord and reaching into the
future to the end of time.

*Teaching men to observe all things whatsoever I
have commanded you*
It is our mission
To be obedient to his teaching:
That the illiterate may read, the young be instructed,
so that the mysteries of the earth's secrets may be shared
with all;
That the sick may be healed, the crippled raised, the
dying comforted, the prisoners freed, the blind restored
to sight;
That the hungry may be fed, the undernourished reclaimed, the unproductive made useful, the dispossessed
defended, the outcast welcomed;
That the rulers may be warned as to the limits of their
power, and the ruled enlightened as to the nature of
their rights.

And lo, I am with you always
It is our mission
To live in fellowship with the Holy Spirit:
That we may know that he precedes us wherever we go,
preparing the path before, opening doors that appear

locked, softening resentment and contempt that seem
unsurmountable;
That we may find him walking at our side, a constant
companion, friend, comforter, initiator;
That we may be sensitive to his direction even though it
lead into conflict, tension, persecution, knowing that so
walked they before us, a noble army of men and women
who planted the gospel in every corner of the world,
and into whose labors we enter.

*And lo, I am with you always, even unto the end of
the world*
It is our mission
To live as if the age would end:
That we may understand the importance of time, that
each act, each day has eternal significance to God;
That we may feel the urgency of this day, that so much
is asked and we have so little to give, that so many are
the dangers yet so many the opportunities;
That we may arise each morn as if this were our last,
prepared to rest our lives, our ambitions, our desires in
him, so that if the night comes and our work is done,
we shall have been faithful stewards;
That we may live in hope, a hope that is in the world
but not bound by the world, a hope that never fails, a
hope that alone gives meaning to our lives, a hope that
gives meaning to all creation.

*Jesus came and spake unto them saying, All power
is given unto me in heaven and in earth. Go ye
therefore and teach all nations, baptizing them in
the name of the Father, and of the Son, and of the
Holy Spirit, teaching them to observe all things
whatsoever I have commanded you: and lo, I am
with you always, even unto the end of the world.*
O Lord, by thy grace help us to be faithful to this, our
mission. *Amen*

148 A LITANY FOR CHRISTIAN MISSIONS

Thanks be to thee, most glorious God, Father, Son, and Holy Spirit, for the revelation of thyself in this our world, and for thy commission to thy Church to proclaim the gospel of Christ to every creature.

For the early disciples who were sent out by Christ, to proclaim the coming of the kingdom,

We praise thee, O God.

for the apostles of the nations who, in obedience to his word, carried the gospel through the world,

We praise thee, O God.

For those missionaries, known and unknown, who first brought the gospel to our ancestors,

We praise thee, O God.

For all who at any time have recalled the Church to her great task of evangelizing the world,

We praise thee, O God.

For those who have gone to the ends of the world with the joyful news, and have sought out the dark places of the earth to bring light to them that dwell in the shadow of death,

We praise thee, O God.

For thy missionary servants who have joined the noble army of martyrs; and for all converts to the faith who have sealed their testimony with their blood,

We praise thee, O God.

For the innumerable company who now praise thy name out of every kindred and nation and tongue,

We praise thee, O God.

We acknowledge, O Lord, that we have proved unworthy of thy mercies, and confess how little we have done to hand on, in freedom and fullness, the faith which was brought to us through many perils and purchased with such pain. And the Church's long neglect of this, her bounden duty,

O Lord, forgive.

Our past unfaithfulness,

O Lord, forgive.

Our neglected opportunities,

O Lord, forgive.

Our deafness to thy calls,

O Lord, forgive.
Our small sacrifice for so great a cause,
  O Lord, forgive.
Our forgetfulness of those who have gone forth relying on our prayers,
  O Lord, forgive.
Our unchristian example at home revealed to the world in our racial prejudices, our narrow nationalism, our wars, and our slums,
  O Lord, forgive.

Stir up, O God, the hearts of thy faithful people to greater obedience, and unite thy Church to face the world's great need. Send forth, we pray thee, laborers into thy harvest; and support by thy presence, guide by thy counsel, and fill with thy power those who have gone forth.

Finally, O Lord, we pray that thou wouldst give to all professing Christians, living in foreign lands, a sense of their responsibility, that they may adorn the doctrine of our Savior, and by their good example commend the faith to others. So do thou hasten the time, O Father, when the gospel shall have been preached to all nations, and the whole world shall be filled with the knowledge of thy love. *Amen*

149 Grant to all missionaries, O God, such grace and humility of spirit as may enable them to learn of those whom they are teaching, and freely to commit to them the care of the Church in their country, that it may increase in strength to accomplish its task. *Amen*

150 Almighty and most merciful God, pour out, we pray thee, abundantly upon the students in our universities and colleges the gift of thy Holy Spirit, that many among them may in these days hear thy voice and offer themselves for the service of thy Church overseas or in neglected parts of our own land, in Christ. *Amen*

Section Four: Special Seasons

[Prayers for the Church Year may be found in appropriate places in Part II, "Bible Study in Worship," where they appear in relation to events in the life of our Lord. Those provided here are supplementary, or they concern seasons not celebrated as part of the Church Year.]

151 THE OPENING OF THE COLLEGE YEAR

Our Father, it is with a sense of peculiar privilege and rare opportunity, that we come to college this fall. Without too much anxiety before an unknown future, and with confidence that thou art able to care for us and to use us in every situation, we would give ourselves to the work now at hand, in the name of Jesus Christ. *Amen*

152 THE ENDING OF THE COLLEGE YEAR

O God, our heavenly Father, we praise thee for the gift of this school year—for its demanding discipline and its healthy freedom; for the joy of effort and the joy of rest; for the inspiration of human friendship and most of all for the friendship of Christ our Lord. May thy presence go with all whose days among us now draw to their close. Preserve them in safety under thy protection; keep them loyal at all times to the ideals they have learned; guide them to the work in life thou hast for them to do; and grant that as faithful stewards, they may freely and generously share with others those good gifts which thou hast here bestowed upon them, to thy glory and the blessing of thy world. *Amen*

153 THE NEW YEAR
Father, as the old year ends and a new year begins, forgive us for the failures of the vanished days, and bless us in whatever we have truly striven for in days that do not die. Keep us from vain regrets, and let us face forward in the light of the best that we have learned. Purge our hearts both of shallow self-confidence and cowardly fears, so that we may know that without thee we can do nothing, but that in thee all things are possible, through Jesus Christ our Lord. *Amen*

154 DAYS OF WASHINGTON AND LINCOLN
O God, we thank thee for the wisdom, skill, and consecration with which many great leaders of our country have led us. We thank thee especially for Washington and Lincoln whose faith was firm and sound and rich, and who ever guided themselves by high religious convictions. O God, may there be in our generation spirits like theirs, that in the future we may not leave our beloved land barren of leaders, and shepherdless in time of great need. *Amen*

155 THE LENTEN SEASON
O Lord our Master, who through the forty days didst forget the body because thy spirit wast caught up in God, teach us with whole hearts to seek the heav-

enly communion, so that being delivered from subjection to the flesh we may be released into the spiritual liberty that belongs to the children of God. In thine own name we ask it. *Amen*

156 **PALM SUNDAY**

O God, whose dearly beloved Son was greeted by the crowd on Olivet with alleluias, but who in that same week was mocked as he went lonely to the cross, forbid that our welcome to him should be in words alone. Help us, we beseech thee, to keep the road open for him into our hearts; and let him find there not another crucifixion, but love and loyalty in which his kingdom may be established evermore. *Amen*

157 **GOOD FRIDAY**

Almighty and most merciful Father, whose power is in love, we bless thee for thine infinite compassion to the sins of men in that thou didst give thy blessed Son Jesus Christ to take upon himself the sufferings of the cross. Make us ashamed of the sins in us which crucify his love afresh, and fill our hearts with thankfulness for the undeserved and everlasting grace by which we are redeemed, through him who is the lord of life for ever. *Amen*

158 **EASTER**

Almighty and everlasting God, who on Easter Day didst turn the despair of the disciples into triumph by the resurrection of Christ who had been crucified, give us faith to believe that every good which has seemed to be overcome by evil, and every love which has seemed to be buried in darkness and in death, shall rise again to life immortal, through the same Jesus Christ who lives with thee for evermore. *Amen*

159 **SPRINGTIME**
Almighty God, our creator and preserver, we thank thee for this springtime, in which thou art renewing the face of the earth and quickening all things. When earth, and air, and sky are full of beauty, proclaiming blessing and praise, our hearts would not be thankless nor our mouths dumb. We bless thee, the all-good, whose mercy is boundless, whose grace is infinite. Thou who carest for the trees and the flowers, ever-living and never-failing Spirit, revive and renew our life, that we may bring forth the fruit of good works, as disciples of him who came to quicken in human hearts the seed of eternal life. *Amen*

160 **MEMORIAL DAY**
O God, we thank thee for the lives, the service, and the sacrifice of those who died for our country. May their memory be precious to us, and may we never forget what they did nor why they did it. They met their test, and gave the last full measure of devotion.

Help us in our day, we beseech thee, to build for them the best kind of memorial in a movement which seeks to remove forever the need of any more sacrifice like that, through the influence of the life and teachings of thy Son, Jesus Christ. *Amen*

161 **SUMMERTIME**
Eternal Goodness, who giveth loveliness to the earth and gladness to the heart, we worship thee. We praise thee for the wonderful life of summer; for the

beauty spread upon the hills, and for the flowers that fill the valleys with sweetness. This day, while the light and music and fragrance call us to rejoice, grant that our minds and souls may be open to all heavenly influences. Spirit of beauty and goodness, come and dwell with us that henceforth our lives may be in accord with thy order, and be well-pleasing in thy sight. *Amen*

162 AUTUMN

Blessed be thou, Father of all mercy, who continuest to pour thy benefits upon us. Age after age the living wait upon thee, and find that of thy faithfulness there is no end, and that thy care is unfailing and unwearying. We praise thee that the mystery by which we are compassed about is a mystery of infinite goodness. Thou hast preserved us through the fourfold year, and bestowed again the plenty of harvest. We would not witness and enjoy thy bounty in vain. Build thine altar in our hearts. O make thy goodness to be health and strength unto us, that we may be dutiful and holy. *Amen*

163 THANKSGIVING DAY

Almighty God, our heavenly Father, whose mercies are without number, and the treasure of whose goodness is infinite, we render thee thanks for all the gifts thou hast bestowed upon us. May mutual love and kindness gladden our feast of thanksgiving to thee. We thank thee:

for thy favor shown unto our fathers, and thy faithfulness continued unto their children;

for the rich land given us for an inheritance, and the great power entrusted to the people;

for the fidelity of men set in authority, and the peace maintained by righteous laws;

for protection from outward dangers, and deliverance
from inward strife;
for an honorable place among the nations, and the opportunity of increasing service to the world.

Keep thou the commonwealth beneath thy care, and
guide the state according to thy will; and thine shall
be the glory and the praise and the thanksgiving, from
generation to generation. *Amen*

164 WINTERTIME

Almighty God, who rulest the changing seasons,
and fulfillest in all thine own unchanging purpose; we bless
thee that beneath all that now in winter seems cold and
dead, thou art keeping safe the hidden germs of life, and
preparing for the days when the earth shall again bud
and blossom, and again bring forth her harvest. And
still thou dost ofttimes clothe all things around us with
the perfection of beauty, when thou sendest forth thy
frost and snow, and fillest the brief day with sunshine,
and makest the night glorious with countless stars. We
thank thee for the shelter and comfort of our homes,
and pray for the kind and compassionate heart toward
all whose lot is harder, and who in poverty or sickness
shrink before the cold. *Amen*

165 CHRISTMAS

Almighty God, whom once the nations worshiped under names of fear, but who hast revealed the
glory of thy love in the face of Jesus Christ, and called
us by him to live with thee as children; fill our hearts,
as we remember his nativity, with the gladness of this
great redemption. We would join in the heavenly song
of Glory to God in the highest, on earth peace, and
goodwill toward men. Every year, as this joyful festival
comes round, may it find the world more and more in

harmony with thy will, which has been made known to us through Jesus Christ our Lord. *Amen*

O Love of God, draw back the bolts of my foolish proud contentment, and open the shut doors of my heart. Here in my soul, narrow and cold and unworthy though it be, repeat the spiritual miracle of Bethlehem. Let me feel that into my humanness the divine has entered, to save me from my sins, and to give me the blessedness of new life in Christ. *Amen*

166   THE CLOSE OF THE YEAR

Almighty Father, as we keep holy time under the deepening shadows of the closing year, we thank thee for all that it hath brought to us of mercy and truth. Receive our sorrow for our sins, and in thine infinite mercy blot them out of the book of thy remembrance. Let not the experiences of our past days be lost upon us. Fix in our minds every lesson of faith and duty which thou hast been teaching us. Take from our hearts every veil that would hide from us the shining of the heavenly light. Grant unto us, before the record of this year has been finished and sealed, a fresh consecration, a very honest and deep desire to live according to thy will, as it has been made known to us in Christ. *Amen*

Section Five: Concerning the Two Sacraments

167   PRAYERS FOR CHRISTIAN BAPTISM

O blessed God, as our life in the gospel begins with invocation of thy holy Trinity, so may it continue and also end, after our earthly pilgrimage, in thee, in the grace of Christ, and in the fellowship of thy Holy Spirit. *Amen*

Deliver us, O Father, from casualness about our own baptism, as that event which proclaims for all to see and

hear, that we are thine indeed, called by thy name, given our citizenship in thy kingdom by the promise of this holy sacrament;
Deliver us from treating Christian baptism as a magic rite, linked with pagan superstition and fancy;
Deliver us from the easy legalism, strange to thy holy gospel, which declares that what man does here can change thine eternal intention of love for all thy children. Grant us zeal and persuasiveness to seek the grace of baptism for all men everywhere. So may the seal of thy Fatherhood be laid upon us all, that we may together acknowledge thy love and grace in Christ. *Amen*

168 A LITANY ON HOLY BAPTISM
Almighty God our Father, whose Spirit cometh not unbidden to our hearts, and who hast set forth tokens and symbols to touch us and show thyself near; we give thee thanks and praise for thy sacrament of holy baptism:
For thine eternal and unutterable purpose, seeking us out before we knew thee, as our loved ones dedicated us unto thee in prayer and hope;
  We render thee glory and praise.
For thy grace in making visible and real the mystery of thy presence, that all might see and know that thou dwellest among men;
  We render thee glory and praise.
For the innumerable witnesses of the past who have stood near in this solemn moment, bequeathing to us the blessing of their own baptism in enduring faith and in the work of their hands;
  We render thee glory and praise.
For thy Church, the Body of thy Son our Lord, which in every place, on every continent and among every people, receives now the children of men into the redeemed family of thy love;
  We render thee glory and praise.
For water, like fire, as the fitting sign of cleansing and purity in the power of thy Holy Spirit;
  We render thee glory and praise.

For all vows, hopefully made for us and by us, that we may grow up in the nurture and admonition of thy Word;
We render thee glory and praise.
For the awesome and joyful truth that, in Christ, thou knowest each of us by name, as a father knoweth his children;
We render thee glory and praise.
For the strength and wonder of that covenant of grace by which we are made strong to acknowledge our eternal kinship with thee;
We render thee glory and praise.
For the promise of thy presence given to each of us born of water and the Spirit, spoken in baptism, and fulfilled in all our continuing walk and conversation;
We render thee glory and praise.
O Lord, wash us clean of our sin and shame, that being reborn in Christ and known by his name, we may be constantly refreshed by that loving grace which seeks every child of thy Spirit in holy baptism. *Amen*

169 PREPARATION FOR THE LORD'S SUPPER

O thou blessed Savior Jesus Christ, who hast given thyself to me in the sacrament of holy communion, keep me in thy faith and favor; as thou livest in me, let me also live in thee. May thy body and blood preserve me in the true faith unto everlasting life. *Amen*

Visit, O Lord, we pray thee, and cleanse our consciences, that thy Son our Lord Jesus Christ, when he cometh, may find in us a dwelling prepared for himself; who liveth and reigneth with thee in the unity of the Spirit, one God, world without end. *Amen*

(Thanksgivings)

How amiable are thy tabernacles, O Lord of Hosts.
For the joy and refreshment of the Church's worship;
for the great family who day by day and week by

week, down the ages, and throughout the world, have found their rest at God's altar.

He steadfastly set his face to go to Jerusalem.

For him who for the joy that was set before him endured the cross;

for the holy supper of his body and blood, instituted in the night on which he was betrayed;

for his humility in being present to feed us in this sacrament.

That they may all be one.

For Jew and Greek, bond and free, male and female who have found their unity through partaking of the one body of Christ;

for those here with whom we shall be at one in sharing this sacrament.

(Penitence)

Wherewithal shall I come?
The sacrifices of God are a broken spirit.

For failure to discern the Lord's Body:

by easy acceptance of its divisions;

by regarding as trivial differences of conviction about this holy sacrament;

by intolerance, and denial of the claim of others to have met Christ at his own table.

For fainting hearts and faithless lives:

by failure to believe in the power of Christ's prayer for the unity of his Church;

by timidity in making some new venture in understanding what is unfamiliar, or fellowship with those from whom we differ.

(Intercessions)

I in them and thou in me, that they may be perfected into one; that the world may know . . .

For the visible unity of the whole Church of God; for the universal mission of the Church of God; for my fellow members of the Student Christian Movement, especially those from whom I am divided by denomination; that we may be one; for myself as I prepare to share this sacrament; for us all, that we may look up into the face of our Savior and live.

[154]

(Bidding)

We come not to this supper as righteous in ourselves; we come to seek our life in Christ. This sacrament is a singular medicine for all poor sick creatures, a comfortable help to weak souls; and our Lord requires no other worthiness on our part but that we unfeignedly acknowledge our sin. Wherefore we confess our unrighteousness, beseeching God to forgive our division, to heal our schisms, and by this sacrament to unite us in the holy Christ and make us acceptable in him.

170 PRAYERS BEFORE SHARING THE SACRAMENT

Almighty and everlasting God, behold we approach the sacrament of thy only-begotten Son, our Lord Jesus Christ. As sick, we come to the physician of life; as unclean, to the fountain of mercy; as blind, to the light of eternal splendor; as needy, to the Lord of heaven and earth; as naked, to the king of glory.

We implore therefore the abundance of thine infinite majesty, that thou wouldst heal our sickness, wash our foulness, enlighten our darkness, enrich our poverty, and clothe our nakedness; that we may receive the king of kings and lord of lords, with such reverence and fear, such contrition and love, such faith and purity, such devotion and humility, as is expedient for the welfare of our souls.

Grant us, we beseech thee, to receive not only the sacrament of the Lord's body and blood, but also the substance and virtue of the sacrament. O most merciful God, grant us so to receive the body of thy only-begotten Son, our Lord Jesus Christ, that we may be incorporated in his mystical body, and ever reckoned among his members.

And, O most loving Father, grant us that whom we purpose to receive under a veil, we may at length behold with open face, even thy beloved Son, who with thee and the Holy Spirit liveth and reigneth, ever one God, world without end. *Amen*

O God, who knowest us to be set in the midst of so many
and great dangers, that by reason of the frailty of our
nature we cannot always stand upright; grant to us such
strength and protection as may support us in all dangers,
and carry us through all temptations: through Jesus
Christ our Lord. *Amen*

O God, whose blessed Son did manifest himself to his
disciples in the breaking of bread; open we pray thee the
eyes of our faith, that we may behold thee in all thy
works. *Amen*

O God, who feedest us thy children with the true manna,
the living bread from heaven; grant, we beseech thee,
that this precious food may be our support throughout
our earthly pilgrimage, until we reach that land where is
neither hunger nor thirst: through Jesus Christ our Lord.
Amen

Section Six: The End of Life, and the Communion of Saints

171 GRACE TO FACE DEATH
O God, who holdest our souls in life, and hast
appointed unto all men once to die; grant that when our
last hour cometh, and the time of our earthly sojourn is
ended, we may be neither troubled nor dismayed; but
that being satisfied with thy goodness and mercy, we may
commend our spirits to thy care; and firmly trusting in
the merits of thy Son, our Savior, obtain a peaceful
death and a happy entrance into the world of light. This
we beg for the sake of him who died for us that we
might live with thee forever. *Amen*

O Lord, support us all the day long of this troublous
life, until the shadows lengthen and the evening comes,
and the busy world is hushed, and the fever of life is
over, and our work is done. Then of thy mercy grant us
a safe lodging, and a holy rest, and peace at the last,
through Jesus Christ our Lord. *Amen*

O God, be near to us when we suffer physical pain and wonder why this affliction should come to us. Assuage our distress and anguish when someone dear to us is taken unto thee. Come to us, O God, when all others leave us, when we feel that no one else understands or cares, and when there seems nothing to go on for. Give us strength and will to withstand the storms that beat against our life, and keep us steadfast, for Jesus' sake. *Amen*

O Lord Jesus Christ, who by thy life hast made us able to believe in a heavenly Father's love, come close to us in our time of agony. Thou who in Gethsemane didst pray to be delivered from the cross, be near us when we must drink our bitter cup of sorrow and of desolation. Thou who in thine own dark hour criedst, My God, my God, why hast thou forsaken me?—hear our cry. Teach us that beyond every Gethsemane and every Calvary there waits a resurrection. Help us to trust when we cannot see; and by the comradeship of thy victorious suffering to know that love and life are everlasting and that God's mercy does not fail. *Amen*

Lord, thou knowest our cares and our fears. Help us to turn them all over to thee, who hast promised to give rest to our souls. Grant to us now a restful spirit and a peaceful mind, and in quietness and confidence to find new strength. *Amen*

Father,
We thank thee that this turmoil, this haste, this shouting
    of many tongues,
Is but for a moment:
That this world passes swiftly away
As the crowd ebbs from a city street.
In the brief moments that remain,
Help us, O our God,
To dwell ever more closely with thee,
Rejecting all lesser goods,
Giving our lives ever more gladly for thy service. *Amen*

172 **FOR ASSURANCE OF IMMORTALITY**

Eternal Love, with whom the souls of the faithful, after they are freed from this mortal flesh, shall abide forever in strength and gladness; we give thee hearty thanks that their bodies also, which have borne the image of the earthy, shall bear the image of the heavenly. Wherefore, having this confidence concerning them that are asleep, we wait with cheerful hope till thou shalt accomplish the number of thine elect, in Christ Jesus. *Amen*

Father and King,
We thank thee that in thyself all spiritual values are
        forever conserved;
That nothing true, noble and pure, in action or in
        character
Can for one moment of all eternity be lost.
But that all such things, being of thy eternal nature,
Forever are treasured and perfected in thyself.
We thank thee that though these our bodies—
These poor vehicles of thy self-expression in human
        goodness, beauty and truth—
Must of necessity fail and be scattered in dust,
Yet the souls that have shown forth thyself
Live forever, perfected and rejoicing, in thee. *Amen*

173 **IN MEMORY OF STUDENTS FALLEN IN WAR**

We give thee humble and hearty thanks, O merciful God, for the lives and examples of thy servants; for their high ideals and aspirations in college days; for their ready response to the call of their country; for their cheerfulness and courage in the midst of suffering and danger; for their steadfastness and self-sacrifice in the hour of death. Grant, O Lord, that the offering of their lives may not have been made in vain, and that we and all thy people may hear the call which sounds in our ears from the graves of those who have died that we might live. So out of the war years of sin and misery and loss, may there by our rededication to thy kingdom arise a better nation and a better world, in Christ. *Amen*

174 IN MEMORY OF GREAT SOULS

We give thanks to thee, O Lord, for all saints and servants of thine, who have done justly, loved mercy, and walked humbly with their God. For all the high and holy ones, who have wrought wonders and been shining lights in the world, we thank thee. For all the meek and lowly ones who have earnestly sought thee in darkness, and held fast their faith in trial, and done good unto all men as they had opportunity, we thank thee.

Especially for those men and women we have known and loved, who by their patient obedience and self-denial, steadfast hope and helpfulness in trouble, have shown the same mind that was in Christ Jesus, we bless thy holy name. As they have comforted and upheld our souls, grant us grace to follow in their steps, and at last to share with them in the inheritance of the saints in light, through Christ our Savior. *Amen*

The World

Section One: Friendship Among Nations

175 THE WORLD'S WRONGDOING OUR OWN
If thou, O Lord, shouldst mark iniquity—O Lord, who would stand? Enter not into judgment with thy servants, for in thy sight is no man living justified. In thy presence, our Father, our disguises and pretenses do not avail, and under the light of thy holiness we know ourselves for what we are: mean and petty creatures who seek our own in spite of our noble pretensions. Have mercy on us. Give us the grace to see our faults more clearly that we may truly repent.

We confess the sorry confusion of our common life to thee. The nations are still at war with one another, each nation seeking its own advantage. Our national life is burdened with the sin of injustice. Millions live in insecurity and poverty while others spend their substance in riotous living. Those who possess authority love power more than justice and use their fellow men as tools of their own desires. The cry of the needy arouses us only slightly from our selfish indifference.

We acknowledge that the world's sin is our own, that the greed which we condemn when it results in obvious inhumanity is in our own heart; that the world is unjust because none of us loves justice with sufficient abandon; that the vices of civilization are compounded of the lusts of all of us. Give us grace to look into our own hearts before we cast a stone of condemnation.

May we achieve the grace of true humility in thy presence, so that we may cease to defeat thy will for the world by our self-will. May the vision of what we might be convict us of what we are, so that thy mercy may redeem us of our sin, through Jesus Christ our Lord. *Amen*

176 FOR TRUE INTERNATIONALISM

Grant, O Lord,

That we may approach every question of foreign policy
from the viewpoint of our Christian faith;

That we may check in ourselves and in others every temper
which makes for war, all ungenerous judgments, all
presumptuous claims, all promptings of self-assertion,
the growths of ignorance and passion;

That we may endeavor to understand the needs, the
feelings, the endowments, the traditional aspirations
of other countries;

That we may do gladly, unweariedly, patiently, what lies
in us to remove suspicions and misunderstandings;

That we may honor all men. *Amen*

177 FOR A UNITING ORGANIZATION OF
NATIONS

Almighty God, who dost call all nations into
thy kingdom and in whose sight all men are equal, we
pray thee to draw together all peoples into a just and
mighty world organization. Destroy the influences, secret
and open, which are fighting against it. Cleanse diplo-
macy and commerce from all that is base and mean. In
the dealings of nation with nation, and men with men,
may goodwill and respect of others take the place of
jealousy and war. Banish cynicism and bring back hope.
Increase our faith in one another and in the power of
thy righteous will; so may justice, mercy, and peace
prevail among the nations, and thy name be glorified,
through Christ. *Amen*

178 FOR WORLD SHARING

God our Father, give to the nations of the
world a new heart of comradeship; that every people
may bring its tribute of excellence to the common treas-

ury, without fear, and without the lust of domination; and that all the world may go forward in the new and living way which he hath consecrated for us who now liveth and reigneth, with thee and the Spirit of truth, one God, world without end. *Amen*

We pray thee, O God, that we may live in reverence for thy bounteous creation, and in all things work for a just sharing of food, shelter, and tools among all men; to the end that starvation, coldness, and loneliness may disappear from the earth, and the work of men be an honor to thee, lifting the dignity of all thy people everywhere. *Amen*

179 A LITANY OF REMEMBRANCE OF ALL PEOPLES

Almighty God, we lift to thee our hopes and prayers for all the peoples of the world; thou knowest their condition and need as we do not, and our thoughts of them are poor because we have not cared enough to seek knowledge of them. Accept thou our prayer as we turn outward the earnestness of our hearts, uniting our wills with thine own mighty intention of good for them:

We remember in silence before thee
The great lands of Africa and the Middle East, ancient home of kings, birthplace of our culture, land of bitter wrongs, of ignorance and fear, of disease and death; yet a land of promise, of great rivers and forests, mountains and plains, eager and strong men and women seeking freedom and thee.

(Silence)

We remember in silence before thee
The peoples of India and all Asia that their divisions may be healed, their emancipation in thee established, and their wisdom increased to accept from other cultures only that which ennobles and exalts.

(Silence)

We remember in silence before thee
The peoples of Latin America, struggling upward from

ignorance and chaos into swift new achievement and promise, yet hampered by tragic failures of government and of enlightenment, that they may find their destiny anew in thy purpose.

(Silence)

We remember in silence before thee

The peoples of Europe and Great Britain, many times crushed by war and borne down with old divisions, that as bearers of the message of Christ they may again be inspired by thy power in all their common life.

(Silence)

We remember in silence before thee

The people of the isles and continents of the seas, whose new civilization has sprung up beside ancient tribal ways, that in a day of swift planes and ships, they may share what is deepest and best in the world's ways.

(Silence)

We remember in silence before thee

Our own peoples on this continent, proud, tireless, groping for new faith even as they seek to live up to the old; that without condescension and overweening trust in their own powers, they may humbly take their part in thy holy pattern for the world's life.

(Silence)

Grant, O God, that our imagination may be stretched to enable us to share the poignant need and also the exultation of men everywhere; that so we may dwell in a large place, and make thy Church strong in every land, in every tongue, for every people, in Christ Jesus. *Amen*

180 FOR A WAY BETTER THAN WAR

O Lord, since first the blood of Abel cried to thee from the ground that drank it, this earth of thine has been defiled with the blood of man shed by his brother's hand, and the centuries sob with the ceaseless horror of war. Ever the pride of kings and the covetousness of the strong has driven peaceful nations to slaughter. Ever the songs of the past and the pomp of armies have been used to inflame the passions of the people.

Grant to us, O God, a quiet and steadfast mind when our own nation clamors for vengeance or aggression. Strengthen our sense of justice and our regard for the equal worth of other peoples and races. May our young men still rejoice to die for their country with the valor of their fathers, but teach our age nobler methods of matching our strength, and more effective ways of giving our life for the flag.

O thou strong Father of all nations, draw all thy great family together with an increasing sense of our common blood and destiny; that peace may come on earth at last, and thy sun may shed its light rejoicing on a holy brotherhood of peoples. Through him who is the Prince of Peace. *Amen*

181   A LITANY FOR WORLD PEACE
(1)

Remember, O Lord, the peoples of the world divided into many nations and tongues; deliver us from every evil which obstructs thy saving purpose; and fulfill thy promises of old to establish thy kingdom of peace:

From the curse of war and all that begets it,
  O Lord, deliver us.
From believing and speaking lies against other nations,
  O Lord, deliver us.
From narrow loyalties and selfish isolation,
  O Lord, deliver us.
From fear and distrust of other nations, from all false pride, vainglory, and self-conceit,
  O Lord, deliver us.
From the lust of the mighty for riches, that drives peaceful peoples to slaughter,
  O Lord, deliver us.
From putting our trust in the weapons of war, and from want of faith in the power of justice and goodwill,
  O Lord, deliver us.

From every thought, word, and deed which divides the human family and separates us from the perfect realization of thy love,

    O Lord, deliver us.

(2)

Eternal Father, who showest thy people the way in which they should go, turn our feet from the city of destruction toward the city of God, and redirect our desires and labors in accordance with thy will; that we may achieve the new world for which thy Son was content to die, even Jesus Christ our Lord.

That nations may vie with each other in the service of man and not in seeking dominion,

    Father, we pray thee.

That science may be the constant handmaid of life and never the henchman of death,

    Father, we pray thee.

That the treasure now spent on the engines of war may be used for the arts of peace,

    Father, we pray thee.

That thy people may rejoice to endure labor and want and death to win, not a war, but thy kingdom,

    Father, we pray thee.

That we may love not only our country but also the whole family of nations,

    Father, we pray thee.

That ancient enmities may pass away and that thou wilt make all things new,

    Father, we pray thee.

(3)

O Christ, at whose word the wind and waves were still, rebuke, we pray thee, the violence of men, and usher in the day of brotherhood; that we may truly serve thee, who with the Father and the Holy Spirit liveth and worketh for us unceasingly, now and forever.

Lord of life, master of men, pattern of gentleness,

    Hear us, Lord Jesus.

By the prophets' dream of old,

    Grant us victory over war.

By the angels' song of peace,

    Raise up leaders of goodwill.

By thy gospel's words of love,
Help us to love our enemies.
By thy sacrificial death,
Teach the nations self-denial.
By the kingdom thou hast promised,
Make the nations one.

(4)

God of the future years, we pray for all thy family upon earth and for every agency of world co-operation that it may grow in usefulness and power:
For thy universal Church,
We beseech thee.
For the world organization of nations,
We beseech thee.
For international federations of labor, industry, and commerce,
We beseech thee.
For the departments of state, for all ambassadors, ministers, diplomats, and statesmen,
We beseech thee.
For the prophets and pioneers who have seen the promised land afar off and dedicated their lives to its service,
We beseech thee.
For the common folk in every land who live in peace and quietness,
We beseech thee.
Eternal Father, unto thee we commit ourselves; use even us with our ignorance and frailty to accomplish thy holy will; and hasten the day when all shall dwell together in mutual helpfulness and love; for thine is the kingdom, the power, and the glory, forever. *Amen*

182 FOUR PRAYERS FOR PEACE

Create peace, O God, to them that are afar off, and peace to them that are nigh. At home and abroad confound the devices of those who trouble thy kingdom; and restrain and foil those who delight to hurt, to avenge, and to destroy. And raise up many peoples in thy fear to be quiet habitations of righteousness, and temples not to be shaken down. *Amen*

Father in heaven, thy children stumble in darkness, and fears deface the plan thou gavest us in thy Son Jesus. Pagan symbols hide the cross, and the proud of the earth proclaim their triumph. In a world looking for conquerors who ride in armed ranks and whose banners are stained with blood, grant us to kneel where the meek of the earth still pray for brotherhood and peace; where homes, not empires, shall wear the crowns. *Amen*

O God, we praise thy name for all who in war have given up their lives for high ideals, and who have shown that self-abandon and courage which must ever be man's dearest possession. As we remember them, keep us, O God, from softness and indolence, from selfishness and the path of least resistance. Whenever we slip into a cheap and easy way, let the trumpets awaken us to the memory of millions whose bodies lie beneath the sod.

Lead each one of us into the warfare of the present, into that stern and holy cause wherein goodwill shall be brought out of blindness and misunderstanding. So may it be that peace may prevail among homes and schools, in shop and factory and mine, among rich and poor, among all nations and races. Suffer us not to stay apart from life's chief battlefield, but make us only sorry we have but one life to give upon it. And grant that in this our service together we may meet thee face to face through Jesus Christ our Lord. *Amen*

183 **PRAYERS FOR OUR ENEMIES**
Most loving Father, who by thy Son Jesus Christ hast taught us to love our enemies and to pray for them; we beseech thee, give to those who have been our enemies the light of thy Holy Spirit; grant that they and we, being enlightened in conscience and cleansed from every sin, may know and do thy will, and so be

changed from foes to friends united in thy service: through Jesus Christ our Lord. *Amen*

God of all men weak and strong, evil and just, white and black, old and young, we bring to thee the warring confusion of our times. In our fellowship we have no enemies; yet as citizens of nations, we take part in war, cold hatred, and world-wide mechanized violence and horror. Show us, O God, that these "enemies" are men and women like ourselves: like us they plan and yearn and dream, like us they are sinful and fall into devious ways; among them are those who are cruel and unthinking, among them the uninformed, the innocent, the brave, and the wistful.

What we ask for them we ask also for ourselves: that thou wilt forgive them their sins, and bring them by thine infinite wisdom and love to truth and justice, sensitiveness and nobility.

Save us all, O Lord, from the sin of war and its bitter enmity; grant to us, and to those against whom our nation struggles, contrite hearts and yielded spirits, that we may together be led toward the day thy blessed kingdom shall be fulfilled. *Amen*

Most merciful and loving Father, who hatest not any of the things which thou hast made, but sufferest and bearest with men's misdoings to lead them to repentance; we beseech thee most humbly to pour out upon our enemies with bountiful hand whatever things thou knowest will do them good, and chiefly a mind whereby they may know thee, and be in charity with us thy children for thy sake. Separate them not from us by punishing them, but join and knit them to us by thy favorable dealing with them. And, seeing we be all ordained to be citizens of the one everlasting city, let us begin by mutual love to enter now into the way that leadeth thither, in Christ. *Amen*

184 A LITANY FOR OUR COUNTRY

O Eternal God, ruler of all the earth, we bless thee for our country. Bountifully hast thou given to us, beyond all our deserving. Thou hast made us heirs of what the untold ages have created: the majesty of upthrust mountains, the green of wooded hills, the prairies rolling to their far horizons, the fertile valleys where the rivers run. All that we can accomplish rests on this which thou hast given. Hear us as we bring to thee the tribute of our grateful hearts:

For all the mighty width of land from bordering sea to sea,

> *We thank thee, O Lord.*

For endless fields where the grain harvests ripen, for orchards with their golden fruit,

> *We thank thee, O Lord.*

For cattle in the meadows, for the wild things in the woods, for the fish in the ocean and lakes and mountain streams, for the homely creatures of the barnyard and for the infinite beauty of winged birds,

> *We thank thee, O Lord.*

For rich ores hidden in the hills, for coal and oil and iron, and for all the treasures of unnumbered mines,

> *We thank thee, O Lord.*

For the strength and skill of all the multitude of toiling men on whom our life depends: on farms, in fishing fleets, in factories, and before the fires of furnaces and mills,

> *We thank thee, O Lord.*

For the genius of inventors, for the imagination of engineers, for the daring of those who have dreamed a mightier civilization and have fashioned their dreams in stone and steel,

> *We thank thee, O Lord.*

For those who laid the railroads and launched the ships and planes, for those who have built the bridges and lifted the towers of cities to the sky,

> *We thank thee, O Lord.*

For all the host of men and women who in industry, in

commerce and in communications hold the world together because they are dependable at their daily posts,
  We thank thee, O Lord.
For all the servants of the mind, for scholars and teachers, for authors and artists, and for all poets in word or
deed who reveal the wideness and wonder of the world,
  We thank thee, O Lord.

Yet we remember that as we have greatly received so in
the same measure we are responsible. Forbid that we
should be recreant to our trust, or that the fire which
has been passed on to us should perish. Help us to be
worthy of our fathers, and of our fathers' God:
To all the high desires of the pioneers and prophets,
  O God, help us to be faithful.
To their belief in the possibilities of common men,
  Help us to be faithful.
To their passion for freedom and their readiness to live
and die in its defense.
  Help us to be faithful.
To their scorn of tyranny, and their trust in men to rule
themselves,
  Help us to be faithful.
To their vision of a human commonwealth in which the
folk from many lands might share,
  Help us to be faithful.
To their release from prejudice and passion of an old
world and their will to build a new,
  Help us to be faithful.
O God, our fathers trusted in thee,
  And were not confounded.
They lifted their faces to thee,
  And were not ashamed.
So enlighten us, O Father, and lead us on thy redeeming
way, through Jesus Christ our Lord. *Amen*

185 O Lord, thou hast dealt favorably with us, and
hast given unto us a pleasant land. We have heard with
our ears, and our fathers have told us what work thou

didst for us in their day, and in the old time before them. But, O God, we are a stiffnecked race, a proud nation, and a people laden with iniquity. Yet we are called by thy name, we have kept thy faith, and we have done thy works. O leave us not, nor forsake us. Establish thy house among us, and exalt it. Revive the witness of our godly forebears. Open our eyes by the old gospel to thy present will. Teach us the path of kind and equal justice, that grievance and envy among us may die away. And grant that beyond the seas our ways may so please the Lord that even our enemies may be at peace with us. And so may the counsel of the Lord be our treasure, and wisdom and knowledge become the stability of our times, and our strength of salvation. *Amen*

186 O God, thou great champion of the outcast and the weak, we bless thee for all that America has meant to the alien folk that have crossed the sea in the past, and for all the patient strength and God-fearing courage with which they have enriched our nation. For all the oppressed afar off who sigh for liberty; for all lovers of the people who strive to break their shackles; for all who dare to believe in democracy and the kingdom of God, make thou our great commonwealth once more a sure beaconlight of hope, and a guide on the path which leads to the perfect union of law and liberty, in Christ. *Amen*

187 God of the nations, we come to thee in humble petition for our nation:

For the honest rights of the men and women who do the labor of the world;

For the clean ambition of upright employers;

For integrity in government and in the halls of legislation;

For places where all the children, rich and poor, can play;

For the care of the sick and the prevention of disease and pain;

For the beauty of the cleansed countryside and the glory of redeemed cities;

For the enrichment of our schools;

For the purity of undefiled religion in our churches:

These, O God, are our desires and our prayer for our nation, in thee. *Amen*

188 Almighty God, our heavenly Father, bless our country that it may be a blessing to the world; grant that our ideals and aspirations may be in accordance with thy will, and help us to see ourselves as others see us. Keep us from hypocrisy in feeling or action. Grant us sound government and just laws, good education, and a clean press, simplicity and justice in our relations with one another, and above all a spirit of service which will abolish pride of place and inequality of opportunity, through Christ. *Amen*

189 O Lord, who hast taught us that the riches of wickedness profit us nothing, deliver us from the slavery of gain, and from an evil concern for our own selves. Bring public corruption to open shame. Cleanse our gold from bloodguiltiness. Be thou our lawgiver and thou our king. Save us from the golden calf, the faithless priest, and the broken law. Bestow thy blessing on our honest labor, and make our diligence fruitful by thy smile. *Amen*

190 We thank thee, O God, for our country: for the strength and skill of men and women whose inventive genius maintains our business and industry; for minds and hands and training which open new doors in the use of natural resources, for business and markets and trade; for all production and distribution in foods, goods, and machines; for all who labor, whether skilled or unskilled, and for the strength of the unions which give them security and status; for every effort by the united voice of the Churches to improve in our day the lot of all who toil.

Save us, O God, from exploitation in our economic life; from greed and callous insensitiveness to the real needs of others far and near; from self-deception and rationalization of willful and acquisitive ways, and from regarding money as an end more precious than human life. May all the peoples of this land, in all their working, their getting and their spending, increasingly know thee whom to know is life eternal. *Amen*

191 O Lord God our Father, guide, we beseech thee, those who bear authority in our towns and cities, that there may be noble streets and open ways therein, that all the skill and beauty of art and craft may be drawn into the service of the common people, for thy glory and the delight of men. *Amen*

192 Eternal God, who in our time hast lifted up our people to power among the nations which it sought not, nor was fully ready to assume, make us able for this hour to which thou hast called us. Grant unto all the people sobriety and maturity of national judgment, delivering us from sentimentality and hysteria. Forbid that our statesmen should play the tense game of military power among the nations, when the stake has become the future welfare of all mankind; rather, enable them to be bold and magnanimous, knowing the mind of the nation and guided by thee to discern and serve the good of all the nations. So may this people in its time of power prove a blessing to all the world, because our freedom and our discipline are rooted deeply in the Lordship of Christ. *Amen*

Section Three: Thy Kingdom Come on Earth

193 A LITANY ON SOCIAL AWARENESS

O God, our Father, who hast made us thy human children as one family in thee, so that what concerns any must concern all, we confess the evils we have done and the good we have left undone. We have spent our strength too often upon the tower of Babel of our own pride, and have forgotten the city that hath the foundations, whose builder and maker is God. We have been guilty of selfishness and strife when we should have learned to build in brotherhood. We have been content that we ourselves should prosper though many might be poor, that a few should feast while multitudes were famished both in body and in soul. O thou who hast taught us that whatsoever we sow that shall we also reap, help us to repent, before thy judgment comes.

For the clouded eyes that see no further than our own advantage,
> *We confess our sin, O Lord.*

For the dulled imagination that does not know what others suffer,
> *We confess our sin, O Lord.*

For the willingness to profit by injustice which we have not striven to prevent,
> *We confess our sin, O Lord.*

For the selfishness which is quick to gain and slow to give,
> *We confess our sin, O Lord.*

[174]

For the unconcern which makes us cry, Am I my brother's keeper?

We confess our sin, O Lord.

But, O thou who art ever merciful, take away the evil of our conscious and unconscious wrongs, forgive us for our unfaithfulness to the vision of thy kingdom, and grant to us a better purpose for the days to come.

From acquiescence in old iniquities,

Save us, O Lord.

From indifference to the human cost of anything we covet,

Save us, O Lord.

From the greed that wastes the resources of this rich earth,

Save us, O Lord.

From the ignorance that wastes the lives of men and women through unemployment, poverty and deprivation,

Save us, O Lord.

From the cruelty which exploits the needy and defenseless,

Save us, O Lord.

From the blasphemy against the spirit which sells the bodies and souls of children to the golden idol of success.

Save us, O Lord.

From false leadership in business and in government, and, above all, from feebleness in the people which lets false leaders rise,

Save us, O Lord.

Unless the Lord build the house,

Their labor is but vain that build it.

Unless the Lord keep the city,

The watchman waketh but in vain.

But he that sitteth upon the throne said

Behold, I make all things new.

Even so, O God, let thy redemptive purposes work through us to build a new and better order on this earth, for the blessing of thy people and the glory of thy name, through Jesus Christ our Lord. *Amen*

Meditation: *Luke 14:16-24,* or *I Corinthians
12:12-27,* or *Ephesians 4:11-16*

(Giving of Thanks)

O Lord, who hast set mankind in families and nations,
binding us by ties of race and ancestry, and enriching us
with common possessions and traditions, unite us in
gratitude and loyalty to thee.

For the rich gifts that thou hast offered us in times of
peace, for social mingling, industrial co-operation and
mutual help,
We thank thee, O God.
For the leisure which allows us to enjoy music and art
and literature,
We thank thee, O God.
For just government, for law and order, and for all good
traditions in our social and business life,
We thank thee, O God.
For our national institutions for the promotion of health
and education, the relief of want, the restraint of evil,
and the assistance of the weak,
We thank thee, O God.
For the increase of social sympathy among us, the grow-
ing indignation against wrongdoing and oppression, the
new discontent with needless suffering and disease,
We thank thee, O God.
For all honest public service for the good of the com-
munity,
We thank thee, O God.
For the promise of the coming of thy kingdom, and the
joy of working for it with our fellow men,
We thank thee, O God.
For all who have been leaders and pioneers, and for all
men and women who have been faithful in the daily
work of life,
We thank thee, O God.

(Penitence)

King of men and Father of our Lord Jesus Christ, who
hast made a great marriage feast for thy Son and sent
forth thy servants to call us that are bidden to it:

We have refused to come. Thou sendest again and again and hast made all things ready. We have made light of thy call and gone our ways, and we have even hurt thy servants.

We that are bidden are not worthy; yet be not very wroth; destroy us not, but send forth thy servants yet again to call us as well as others to the feast.

And grant that we, repenting and turning, the one from his ease, the other from his business, may yet be found by them in the highways and constrained to come in to that great supper of the Lamb. *Amen*

(Petition)

From deafness to thy call and preoccupation with self-chosen ends,

Deliver us, good Lord.

From slackness in seeking thy will for ourselves and others,

Deliver us, good Lord.

From self-seeking and indifference to others in the work of earning a living,

Deliver us, good Lord.

From conformity to the world, and contentment with less than the best,

Deliver us, good Lord.

From neglect to hallow the common life of business,

Deliver us, good Lord.

From pride of class or race, from carelessness of speech and action, and from all contempt of others,

Deliver us, good Lord.

That a wise and humble spirit may prevail in our Congress and legislatures, and all our courts and councils; that those who bear rule may be delivered from unscrupulous ambition, selfish rivalries, and mistaken judgments.

Bless us and lift us up, O God.

That our soldiers and sailors, marines and airmen may be defended amid the dangers and temptations of their calling, and that the nations may live together in peace and charity,

Bless us and lift us up, O God.

That the unspeakable power which thou hast given over into the hands of man, unlocking the might of the atom

and the secrets of matter for violence or for blessing,
may be used as a holy trust for all mankind,
Bless us and lift us up, O God.
That parents may train up their children in right ways;
and that children may be taught to face and grapple
with the evil that is in the world, and grow up a generation to love and praise thee,
Bless us and lift us up, O God.
That men of wealth and ease may not miss the true end
of life; that men of poor and humble lot may keep their
self-respect and be preserved from misery and bitterness
of soul,
Bless us and lift us up, O God.
That social life and industry may be so ordered that
one man's good may not be another man's hurt, and
that all may have their fair share of wealth and freedom,
Bless us and lift us up, O God.
That men and women may eagerly respond to every call
to sacrifice and service, so that the ends of the earth may
see thy salvation,
*Bless us and lift us up, O God, and redeem this thy
world by thy grace and our humble service in thee.
Amen*

195 FOR NEW STIRRINGS OF WORLD FREEDOM
O God, there are sounds on the earth and signs
in the heaven that quicken all hearts with expectation:

nations that long have sat in darkness and the shadow
of death, turning to the light;
peoples that long have worn the yoke of tyranny rising
to shake themselves free;
murmurs of the masses too long content with slavery;
thoughts that threaten the order of all things and predict the shaking of the foundations of the world.

We listen to hear if these are the sounds of thy chariot
wheels; we lift our heads to see if the dawn is reddening
in the sky.

We dare to watch for thy fuller coming to us. For the complete manifestation of thyself, for the emancipation of humanity from fear, sin, doubt and despair.
We dare to pray that thou shouldst make thine entrance through our hearts. Even so, Lord Jesus: come quickly. *Amen*

196 **A CONFESSION OF WRONG IN OUR SOCIETY**
Almighty and most merciful Father, we have erred and strayed from thy ways like lost sheep.

We have strayed from our own responsibilities to families and communities thinking we would thus be free.

We have followed too much the devices and desires of our own hearts.

We have been too sentimental and at the same time have followed too much the logic of our minds; we have built great universities to search out truth, then hidden behind their ivied walls protecting ourselves from strife and danger.

We have offended against thy holy laws.

We have allowed our communities and nations to respect selfishness and injustice and have washed our hands of the "due process of law."

We have left undone those things which we ought to have done.

We have been irresponsible in our economic life and allowed unrighteousness to hold sway in politics and the struggle for power.

And we have done those things which we ought not to have done.

We have lived at the expense of our poorer brothers at home and abroad; we have used the terrible destructiveness of science against our enemies.

And there is no health in us.

There is conflict in the depths of our souls which has driven us into sickness of mind and body.

But thou, O Lord, have mercy upon us, miserable offenders,

Who have considered ourselves untainted by the evil of our modern world.

Spare thou those, O God, who confess their faults,

Be they personal, social, cultural or religious sins.

Restore thou those who are penitent

And would change both themselves and their society

According to thy promises declared unto mankind in Christ Jesus our Lord

Through whom together we are raised up into thy kingdom on earth and in heaven.

And grant, O most merciful Father, for his sake, that we may hereafter live a godly, righteous, and sober life

Ordered by thy law and freed by thy grace.

To the glory of thy holy name. *Amen*

197 FOR ALL WHO ARE IN NEED

O God, in deep compassion we pray thee this day for all the people of this earth:

for homes near and dear to us;

(Silence)

for those who have gone out from our homes to guard the freedom of the earth, that they may have strength and courage;

(Silence)

for those who work long weary hours in field and factory, providing food and clothing for the needs of mankind;

(Silence)

for all those who do not understand the days of our years, and who walk perplexed and bewildered, taking no effective part in the life of men because they do not understand;

(Silence)

for all conquered peoples who must await in agony the day of their deliverance;

(Silence)

most of all, for those who have lost the vision of human brotherhood, whose feet walk the paths of delusion and darkness which lead not into life or truth.

(Silence)

Redeem us, O Lord, by thy grace, that we may devote every ounce of our power in life to the service of all those who can be liberated by thy love. *Amen*

198   SHARE THE WORK OF SOCIAL REDEMPTION

We pray thee, O Lord, for the graces of a pure and holy life, that we may no longer add to the dark weight of the world's sin that is laid upon thee, but may share with thee thy redemptive work. Fill us now with hunger and thirst for justice, that we may bear glad tidings to the poor, and set at liberty all who are in the prison house of want and sin. Help us in patience to carry forward the eternal cross of thy Christ, counting it joy if we, too, are sown as grains of wheat in the furrows of the world. For thou hast shown us, O Father, that only by the agony of the righteous comes redemption. *Amen*

199   DELIVERANCE FROM COMPLACENCY

O Lord, we pray that thou wilt hasten the time when no man shall live in contentment while he knows that his neighbor has need. Inspire in us and in all men the consciousness that we are not our own, but thine and our neighbors'; for his sake who prayed that we might all be one in him. *Amen*

200   DELIVERANCE FROM INTOLERANCE

O God, forgive us for the way we have placed shackles about religion, for the intolerance we have shown toward those who think not as we do, for our refusal to understand the birthpangs of new life all about us. Deepen our sense of the sacredness of every realm of human knowledge and experience. May we approach all new discovery with humility. Amid the intoxication of new ideas, may we never forget to be kind, generous, unselfish, knowing that he that loveth sincerely is most surely born of God. *Amen*

201 **DELIVERANCE FROM ANTI-SEMITISM**
Lord God of Israel, and of the prophets of all ages and of all nations, by all that we have received of the Jews, make us mindful of our debt. We have shut these thy people often from our friendship, and strangled the aspirations in their hearts by our coldness and prejudice. Cleanse our hearts from secret faults, and take not thy Holy Spirit from us. *Amen*

202 **DELIVERANCE FROM RACISM**
Lord of life, who hast made of one blood all races of men to dwell on the face of the earth, save us from all contempt and resentment toward those whose color or lineage is unlike our own. Forgive us, O God, the ghettos, the slavery, the savage exploitation, and the casual belittlement of our human brethren in the past. Even as we seek to win all men to faith in Christ, enable us by that faith to honor their dignity and to love them from our hearts. *Amen*

203 **DELIVERANCE FROM THE LIQUOR TRAFFIC**
O God, bring nigh the day when all men shall face their daily tasks with minds undrugged and with tempered passions; when the unseemly mirth of drink

[182]

shall seem a shame to all who hear and see; when the trade that debauches men shall be loathed like the trade that debauches women; and when all this black remnant of savagery shall haunt the memory of a new generation but as an evil dream of the night. For this accept our vows, O Lord, and grant thine aid. *Amen*

204 DELIVERANCE FROM ISOLATIONISM

O God of truth and law, whose service is perfect freedom, help us to know thy law and find thy truth, that in days of slavery and darkness and oppression on the earth, we may see a light shining along the way that leads mankind to better days. Help us to fit ourselves to take more than an onlooker's part in the struggles of the peoples, that through the light which we have seen there may be more abundant life. Hear our prayer, and answer us according to thy will. *Amen*

205 DELIVERANCE FROM INSENSITIVENESS

Merciful Father, we come to thee confessing the sins of our civilization, in which we all have shared. We have been so bent upon our selfish ends that we would not stop to have mercy. When we have seen those whom the injustices of the world have bruised and beaten, we have passed by on the other side. We have built around ourselves the walls of privilege, within which we might not hear the passion of exploited men, the weeping of women, the bitter cry of children robbed of happy youth.

O God of truth, make us understand.

O God of judgment, wake us to repentance.

O God of mercy, make us fit to ask for thy forgiveness, before it is too late. *Amen*

A LITANY ON THE RIGHTS OF MAN

[Quoting the substance of A Bill of Human Rights agreed upon by the leading nations at mid-century]

Almighty Lord, by whose holy urging the nations in our day, even while at war with each other, have sought a new world order of abiding law; grant to thy Church everywhere insight to see this as thy doing, and vigor to devote heart and mind to this great hope. So may the message of thy love, which has freed men in every age, pervade and redeem even our halting efforts toward world agreement, to the end that all the earth may discover and share the witness of thy grace.

We thank thee, Lord, for the gifts of wisdom and practicality by which leaders of the nations have set forth precepts to establish righteousness: as we dedicate these precepts anew to thy glory, we dedicate ourselves also as instruments of thy high purpose, bringing them to sound expression in the life of every people:

Everyone has the right to life, liberty, and the security of person.
> *Bless all thy people, Lord, that they may know this holy freedom grounded in thy gospel.*

No one shall be held in slavery or servitude; slavery and the slave trade shall be prohibited in all their forms.
> *Bless all thy people, Lord, that they may know this holy freedom grounded in thy gospel.*

No one shall be subjected to torture or to cruel, inhuman or degrading treatment or punishment.
> *Bless all thy people, Lord, that they may know this freedom grounded in thy gospel.*

Everyone has the right to recognition everywhere as a person before the law.
> *Bless all thy people, Lord, that they may know this freedom grounded in thy gospel.*

No one shall be subjected to arbitrary interference with his privacy, family, home or correspondence, nor to attacks upon his honor and reputation.
> *Bless all thy people, Lord, that they may know this freedom grounded in thy gospel.*

Everyone has the right to a nationality.

Bless all thy people, Lord, that they may know this freedom grounded in thy gospel.

Everyone has the right to rest and leisure, including reasonable limitation of working hours and periodic holidays with pay.

Bless all thy people, Lord, that they may know this freedom grounded in thy gospel.

Everyone has the right to a standard of living adequate for the health and well-being of himself and of his family, including food, clothing, housing and medical care and necessary social services, and the right to security in the event of unemployment, sickness, disability, widowhood, old age, or other lack of livelihood in circumstances beyond his control. Motherhood and childhood are entitled to special care and assistance; all children, whether born in or out of wedlock, shall enjoy the same social protection.

Bless all thy people, Lord, that they may know this freedom grounded in thy gospel.

Everyone has the right to education. Education shall be free, at least in the elementary and fundamental stages; elementary education shall be compulsory. Technical and professional education shall be made generally available, and higher education shall be equally accessible to all on the basis of merit.

Bless all thy people, Lord, that they may know this freedom grounded in thy gospel.

Education shall be directed to the full development of the human personality, and to the strengthening of respect for human rights and fundamental freedoms.

Bless all thy people, Lord, that they may know this freedom grounded in thy gospel.

Everyone has the right freely to participate in the cultural life of the community, to enjoy the arts, and to share in scientific advancement and its benefits.

Bless all thy people, Lord, that they may know this freedom grounded in thy gospel.

Men and women of full age, without any limitation of race, nationality, or religion, have the right to marry and to found a family; the family is the natural and fundamental group unit of society, and is entitled to protection by society and the state.

Bless all thy people, Lord, that they may know this freedom grounded in thy gospel.

EVERYONE HAS DUTIES TO THE COMMUNITY, IN WHICH ALONE THE FREE AND FULL DEVELOPMENT OF HIS PERSONALITY IS POSSIBLE.

O God, show us the solemn link between liberties and duties, that our responsibilities may equal our rights in society, and that great eagerness to serve may balance our expectation to be served. So may thy kingdom come in freedom and in discipline, and thy name be glorified in all justice and truth. *Amen*

207 FOR PERSONAL COMMITMENT TO SOCIAL CHANGE

O thou God of infinite horizons, and of patient, toiling love, lift us out of ourselves—out into the battle for the right in city and Church and state; out where greed, poverty, misunderstanding, and ignorance take their toll; out among the needs of those close at hand, for kindness, courage, self-control. Keep us from retreating from men. Make even faster the ties that bind us to the whole human race. So may we be found more truly in the company of Christ. *Amen*

O God, so burn into our hearts the realization of human need, that we shall not dare to be selfish or un-caring as we stand with bowed heads in thy presence. Make us to know that weak and imperfect as we are, we ourselves are instruments thou hast chosen to employ for the world which thou wouldst build. Give us a deep sense of our obligation to seek thy will and to know thine empowering, that our lives may not be wasted in this world. *Amen*

[186]

Lord, give me the serenity to accept what cannot be changed,
Give me the courage to change what ought to be changed,
And the wisdom to know the one from the other. *Amen*

PART IV. GENERAL PRAYERS

PART IV. GENERAL PRAYERS

Litanies

208 AN ACT OF PRAISE
Let us praise God:

For the day, for the glory and warmth of the sun, for the stir of life, and for honest toil that wins food and rest.
God be praised for the day.
For the earth, the sustainer of life; for the hills, the plains, and the dales; and for the beauty of meadows and fields, of flowers and of trees.
God be praised for the earth.
For the sky, for the shifting clouds, and for the glory of sunrise and sunset.
God be praised for the sky.
For the sea, that yields and receives again the water without which life would die, and is wonderful in its stillness and more wonderful in its storm.
God be praised for the sea.

Let us praise God:
For our food, and the pleasure he has given us in it, lest we should neglect the needs of life; may he help us to shun all waste and to rejoice in sharing with others.
God be praised for our food.
For the shelter from wind and weather, which hallowed by love becomes our home; may he strengthen our will that no one shall go hungry or ill-housed or ill-clad.
God be praised for our home.

Let us praise God:
For our fathers and mothers, by whom he orders lives and comforts hearts, bringing strength to a house and sweetness to labor; may he hallow their work and direct their ways.
God be praised for good fathers and mothers.
For the gift of children; may he help us to train them

to be reverent and truthful, that they may gladden our hearts and bring joy to the world.

God be praised for children.

For good friends to rejoice with us in our joys, to cheer us in trouble and to lighten our tasks; may he help us to repay them in fellowship and service.

God be praised for our friends.

Let us praise God:
For joy that heightens all our life and doubles our powers; may he help us to kindle it in the hearts of others by the gladness of our face.

God be praised for joy.

For mirth, that unites us with others and refreshes us for our work; may he help us to keep it kind and true.

God be praised for mirth.

For health, bringing wholesomeness of body and mind; may he help us to give our strength to his service.

God be praised for health.

(A period of silence)

Let us praise God for life.

All praise be to God. Amen

209 **A LITANY OF THE INCARNATION**
O Jesus Christ, the Lord of all good life, who hast called us to build the city of God, do thou enrich and purify our lives and deepen in us our discipleship. Help us daily to know more of thee, and through us, by the power of thy Spirit, show forth thyself to other men. Make us humble, brave, and loving; make us ready for adventure. We do not ask that thou wilt keep us safe, but that thou wilt keep us loyal; who for us didst face death unafraid, and dost live and reign for ever and ever.

From lack of reverence for truth and beauty; from prejudice and sentimentalism; from being contented with the mean and ugly,

O Christ, deliver us.

From the cowardice that dare not face new truth, the laziness contented with half-truths, and the arrogance that thinks it knows all truths,

O Christ, deliver us.

From all kinds of artificiality in life and worship and ministering; from all that is hollow, unreal, and insincere,

O Christ, deliver us.

From trivial ideals and cheap pleasures; from mistaking coarseness and vulgarity for humor,

O Christ, deliver us.

From being dull and pompous; from being rude and offensive and ill-mannered,

O Christ, deliver us.

From the blasphemy of cynicism about our brethren made in the image of God; from all false pride, intolerance, and contempt,

O Christ, deliver us.

From all uncleanness and unwholesomeness; from selfishness, slackness, and self-indulgence,

O Christ, deliver us.

From the false piety which cannot laugh; from being self-centered in our pity; from being narrowly ecclesiastical; and from loving systems more than we love thee,

O Christ, deliver us.

From the disloyalty of being dissatisfied with things as they are, in the Church and in the world; and from failing to share thy indignation,

O Christ, deliver us.

From everything in our lives and methods which may hide the true light of thee, who art the light of the world,

O Christ, deliver us.

O Eternal God, who in Jesus Christ thy Son hast shown us the revelation of thy character; help us in him to see thee as thou art, and to walk in the way which he has declared to us; who liveth and reigneth with thee and the Holy Spirit now and ever. *Amen*

210 O thou who makest the stars and turnest the shadow of death into the morning, we render thee, our Lord and king, the tribute of our praise:

By all thy works; by thy wonders in heaven and on earth; by the order which reigns over all; by the beauty which shines through all; by the bounty which blesses all:

Teach us, and lead us ever nearer to thee.

By the remembrance of thine ancient mercies; by the revelation of thyself to saints of old; by every holy record of wisdom and piety; by every faithful word of thy servants, and by every good example:

Teach us, and lead us ever nearer to thee.

By the memory of thy Son our Savior, the brightness of thy glory and the image of thy person; by his life and teaching; by his passion and cross; by his heavenly exaltation and the influence of his spirit:

Teach us, and lead us ever nearer to thee.

By the Church of Jesus Christ; by its holy ordinances, offices, and ministries; by its Sunday worship and teaching; by all its seasons of meditation and prayer, and by all the associations of the house of God:

Teach us, and lead us ever nearer to thee.

By the kindness and love thou hast shown us from the beginning of our days until now; by the relations of home; by the love of little children; by the affection and fidelity of friends; by the trials and bereavements which chasten and hallow our earthly love; and by all the memories of our dead:

Teach us, and lead us ever nearer to thee.

By the conflict of our souls with temptation; by our falls and failures; by our shame and repentance; by every holy aspiration, striving, and victory:

Teach us, and lead us ever nearer to thee.

By all the experience and discipline of life; by health and sickness; by success and disappointment; by joy and sorrow; by all the chances and changes of our passing days:

Teach us, and lead us ever nearer to thee.

In all time of our wealth, and in all time of our tribulation; in every circumstance and in every place; in life and in death, O most merciful God, our Father and Redeemer:

Teach us, and lead us ever nearer to thee. Amen

A LITANY FOR PURPOSE AND INSIGHT

211   God of wisdom, who guidest thy sons and daughters through days of preparation, because of the plan thou hast in store for them to serve their fellow men, grant us the joy of discovery, discipline of the mind, friends who share high ideals and, above all, a clear vision of service.

O thou who art never weary of setting us free from the bonds with which we have bound ourselves, we pray for the quiet mind, to bring insights deep into the heart of life, and discernment always clear between the lower and the higher path:

O God, grant us the quiet mind.

We pray thee for enlightened imagination and sympathy, by which we may penetrate the pasteboard scenery of this world, there to perceive the beauty that is deeper than outer form, and the goodwill hidden by the outer shell men wear to keep their heart from being wounded:

O God, grant us imagination enlightened by sympathy.

We pray thee for stalwart courage to match this hour. We did not choose to be born and live in such a day, but thou didst choose to appoint our lives for these demanding years: deliver us from fear and melancholy, and make us glad to share a part of the world's burden in our time:

Grant us stalwart courage.

O God, who hast for each one of us higher hopes than we dare hold for ourselves, make us thoughtful and reverent as we balance the wisdom forever old with knowledge forever new:

Grant us wisdom and knowledge.

So as we discover, with increase of our powers, that all earnest searching leads us to thee, may it stir us also to abide by thy will, that we may inherit thy gifts of purpose and peace of mind, in Christ. *Amen*

212 A LITANY ON THE WORK OF GOD'S SPIRIT
O Lord, who hast set before us the great hope that thy kingdom shall come on earth, and hast taught us to pray for its coming, make us ever ready to thank thee for the signs of its dawning, and to pray and work for that perfect day when thy will shall be done on earth as it is in heaven. For the work of thy Spirit within and beyond the bounds of thy visible Church,
We thank thee, O Lord.
For the work of thy Spirit in the history of the world, through peaceful advance, and through pain and tumult,
We thank thee, O Lord.
For the work of thy Spirit in the history of our own country, through its heroes and leaders, in statecraft, law, and industry,
We thank thee, O Lord.
For the work of thy Spirit in science and commerce, in literature and art,
We thank thee, O Lord.
For the work of thy Spirit in the slow triumph of truth over error,
We thank thee, O Lord.
For the work of thy Spirit in the growing desire for true brotherhood, between men of every class and nation,
We thank thee, O Lord.
For the work of thy Spirit in the spread of education, and in the development of a fuller life for individuals, with healthier surroundings and better conditions,
We thank thee, O Lord.
For the work of thy Spirit in the deepening sense of human worth in all nations and classes, and in the growing reverence for womanhood and childhood,
We thank thee, O Lord.
For the work of thy Spirit in the Church, which will not cease till it joins all nations and kindreds and tongues

and peoples into one great family, to thy praise and glory,

We thank thee, O Lord. Amen

213 A LITANY OF REMEMBRANCE AND DEDICATION

O God of all the agelong yesterdays and of the infinite tomorrows, give us new faith, new hope, new power.

Lift us to thy will, O Lord.

O thou who when the earth was without form and void didst breathe thy Spirit through the darkness, come with thy new creation to the chaos of our present world.

Lift us to thy will, O Lord.

O thou, who didst touch the prophets' lips with fire, send us thy prophets for the days ahead.

Lift us to thy will, O Lord.

O thou, to whom the heroes and the martyrs lifted up their eyes, give us the courage of heroic purpose now.

Lift us to thy will, O Lord.

O thou who from the ranks of common humankind hast taken men and women and refined them with the holy flame, so that in every age those whom the world accounted least have become great; grant to us, the people, responsiveness to noble leadership, and the will to follow it even upon difficult and costly ways.

Lift us to thy will, O Lord.

And especially we pray thee for the Church: Grant that it may be worthy of the name of Jesus. Keep it from cowardice and compromise, and from the subtle corruption of falsely bought success. May it not be conformed to this world, but more and more transformed by the indwelling mind of Christ; until it shall become indeed the body through which his spirit is expressed.

Lift us to thy will, O Lord.

For great visions dawning already in our world,
    We thank thee.

For belief in human brotherhood and for the will to make it true,

We thank thee.

For all men and women who will follow that hope in spite of postponement, persecution, and pain,

We thank thee.

For the seers who go before the crowd and climb the hilltop while yet we grope within the valley,

We thank thee.

For those who have dared and endured and triumphed in the power of an endless life,

We thank thee.

For those who in the radiance of their living have brought into our world the witness of the higher world in which their souls have dwelt; for their humor and their gaiety; for the laughter that made them seem lighthearted, even when they bore the burdens of mankind; for their sympathy and their tenderness; for their compassion to the weak, and their challenge to the strong; for the joyous abundance of their self-giving; and for all their shining witness to their Master, Jesus Christ,

We thank thee, O holy, blessed, and glorious God.

O Christ, Revealer of the Father,

Reveal thyself in us.

O Christ, who didst illumine the darkness of men's despair,

Make us believe in light.

O Christ, who dared to seem defeated on the cross,

Make us believe in love.

O Christ, invincible in sacrifice, risen and immortal,

Make us believe in God triumphant in all life.

And unto God the Father, God the Son, and God the Holy Spirit, be ascribed all might, majesty, dominion, and power, both now and evermore. *Amen*

Prayers of the Great Tradition

214 A GENERAL THANKSGIVING

Almighty God, Father of all mercies, we, thine unworthy servants, do give thee most humble and hearty thanks for all thy goodness and loving-kindness to us, and to all men. We bless thee for our creation, preservation, and all the blessings of this life; but, above all, for thine inestimable love in the redemption of the world by our Lord Jesus Christ; for the means of grace, and for the hope of glory. And, we beseech thee, give us that due sense of all thy mercies, that our hearts may be unfeignedly thankful; and that we show forth thy praise, not only with our lips, but in our lives, by giving up ourselves to thy service, and by walking before thee in holiness and righteousness all our days; through Jesus Christ our Lord, to whom, with thee and the Holy Spirit, be all honor and glory, world without end. *Amen*

215 A GENERAL CONFESSION

Almighty and most merciful Father, we have erred, and strayed from thy ways like lost sheep. We have followed too much the devices and desires of our own hearts. We have offended against thy holy laws. We have left undone those things which we ought to have done; and we have done those things which we ought not to have done; and there is no health in us. But thou, O Lord, have mercy upon us, miserable offenders. Spare thou those, O God, who confess their faults. Restore thou those who are penitent, according to thy promises declared unto mankind in Jesus Christ our Lord. And grant, O most merciful Father, for his sake, that we may hereafter live a godly, righteous, and sober life, to the glory of thy holy name. *Amen*

216 A PRAYER FOR PURITY

Almighty God, unto whom all hearts are open, all desires known, and from whom no secrets are hid; cleanse the thoughts of our hearts by the inspiration of thy Holy Spirit, that we may perfectly love thee, and worthily magnify thy holy name; through Christ our Lord. *Amen*

217 GOD READIER TO HEAR THAN WE TO PRAY

Almighty and everlasting God, who art always more ready to hear than we to pray, and art wont to give more than either we desire or deserve; pour down upon us the abundance of thy mercy, forgiving us those things whereof our conscience is afraid, and giving us those good things which we are not worthy to ask, but through the merits and mediation of Jesus Christ, thy Son, our Lord. *Amen*

218 FROM COLDNESS OF HEART

O Almighty God, from whom every good prayer cometh, and who pourest out on all who desire it the spirit of grace and supplication; deliver us, when we draw nigh to thee, from coldness of heart and wanderings of mind, that with steadfast thoughts and kindled affections we may worship thee in spirit and in truth: through Jesus Christ our Lord. *Amen*

219 FOR FORGIVENESS

Almighty and most merciful God, we acknowledge and confess that we have sinned against thee in thought, and word and deed; that we have not loved thee with all our heart and soul, with all our mind and strength; and that we have not loved our neighbor as ourselves. We beseech thee, O God, to be forgiving to what we have been, to help us to amend what we are, and of thy mercy to direct what we shall be, so that the love of goodness may ever be first in our hearts and we may follow unto our life's end in the steps of Jesus Christ our Lord. *Amen*

220 **INSTRUMENTS OF THY PEACE**
Lord, make us instruments of thy peace.
Where there is hatred, let us sow love;
    where there is injury, pardon;
    where there is discord, union;
    where there is doubt, faith;
    where there is despair, hope;
    where there is darkness, light;
    where there is sadness, joy;
for thy mercy and for thy truth's sake. *Amen*

221 **WHERE TRUE JOYS ARE TO BE FOUND**
O Almighty God, who alone canst order the unruly wills and affections of sinful men; grant unto thy people, that they love the thing which thou commandest, and desire that which thou dost promise; that so, among the sundry and manifold changes of the world, our hearts may surely there be fixed, where true joys are to be found; through Jesus Christ our Lord. *Amen*

222 **BEGUN, CONTINUED, AND ENDED IN THEE**
Direct us, O Lord, in all our doings, with thy most gracious favor, and further us with thy continual help; that in all our works begun, continued, and ended

in thee, we may glorify thy holy name, and finally, by thy mercy, obtain everlasting life; through Jesus Christ our Lord. *Amen*

223 **WHOSE SERVICE IS PERFECT FREEDOM**

O God, who art the author of peace and lover of concord, in knowledge of whom standeth our eternal life, whose service is perfect freedom; defend us thy humble servants in all assaults of our enemies, that we, surely trusting in thy defense, may not fear the power of any adversaries: through the might of Jesus Christ our Lord. *Amen*

224 **WHEN TWO OR THREE ARE GATHERED**

Almighty God, who hast given us grace at this time with one accord to make our common supplications unto thee; and dost promise that when two or three are gathered together in thy name thou wilt grant their requests; fulfill now, O Lord, the desires and petitions of thy servants, as may be most expedient for them, granting us in this world knowledge of thy truth, and in the world to come life everlasting. *Amen*

225 **HEARTS SET TO OBEY THY COMMANDMENTS**

O God, from whom all holy desires, all good counsels, and all just works do proceed; give unto thy servants that peace which the world cannot give, that our hearts may be set to obey thy commandments, and also that by thee, we, being defended from the fear of our enemies, may pass our time in rest and quietness, through the merits of Jesus Christ our Savior. *Amen*

226 **FOR A NEW SPIRIT**
Almighty and everlasting God, who hatest nothing that thou hast made, and dost forgive the sins of all those who are penitent; create and make in us new and contrite hearts, that we, worthily lamenting our sins and acknowledging our wretchedness, may obtain of thee, the God of all mercy, perfect remission and forgiveness, through Jesus Christ our Lord. *Amen*

227 **GRANT US SO TO KNOW THEE**
Eternal God, the light of the minds that know thee, the joy of the hearts that love thee, and the strength of the wills that serve thee; grant us so to know thee that we may truly love thee, so to love thee that we may fully serve thee, to the honor and glory of thy holy name. *Amen*

Various Other Prayers

228 THANKS FOR BEAUTY AND JOY
Creator of life and light,
We bless thee this day for the beauty of thy world,
For sunshine and flowers, storm cloud and starry night,
For the first radiance of dawn and the last smoldering
glow of the sunset.

We thank thee for physical joy,
For the ecstasy of swift motion,
For deep water to swim in,
For the goodly smell of rain on dry ground,
For hills to climb, and hard work to do,
For all skill of hand and eye,
For music that lifts our hearts in one breath to heaven,
For the handgrasp of a friend,
For the gracious loveliness of children.

We thank thee, above all, for spiritual beauty and joy,
For home love, for mother love, for child love,
For the instant assent of our hearts
To the truth that is spoken by prophet or poet,
For the exceeding bliss of the touch of thy hand,
Awakening suddenly our drowsy souls
Into blessed awareness of thy presence with us and in us:
For all these thy sacraments of beauty and joy
We thank thee our Lord and our God. *Amen*

229 FOR DAILY BLESSINGS
Now unto thee, O heavenly Father, be all
praise and glory that day by day thou dost richly fill my
life with various blessings:
A home to share, kindred to love, and friends to cherish:
A place to fill and a work to do:

A green world to live in, blue skies above me, and pure air to breathe:

Healthy exercise and simple pleasures:

My race's long history to remember and its great men to follow:

Good books to read and many arts and crafts to delight in:

So much that is worth knowing and the skill and science to know it:

Those high thoughts that sometimes fill my mind and come I know not whence:

Many happy days, and that inward calm that thou givest me in days of gloom:

The peace, passing understanding, that comes from thine indwelling in my soul:

The faith that looks through death and the hope of a larger life beyond the grave. *Amen*

230 FOR THE FULLNESS OF LIFE

O Lord, my Lord,
for my being, life, reason,
for nurture, protection, guidance,
for education, civil rights, religion,
for thy gifts of grace, nature, fortune,
for redemption, regeneration, catechizing,
for my call, recall, yea, many calls besides,
for thy forbearance, long-suffering,
long long-suffering,
to me-ward,
many seasons, many years, up to this time:
for all good things received, successes granted me,
good things done;
for the use of things present,
for thy promise, and my hope
of the enjoyment of good things to come;
for my parents honest and good,
teachers kind,
benefactors never to be forgotten,

hearers thoughtful,
friends sincere,
domestics faithful,
for all who have advantaged me,
by writings, homilies, converse,
prayers, patterns, rebukes, injuries,
for all these, and all others
which I know, which I know not,
open, hidden,
remembered, forgotten,
done when I wished, when I wished not,
I confess to thee and will confess,
I bless thee and will bless,
I give thanks to thee and will give thanks,
all the days of my life. *Amen*

231 **FOR A NEW WEEK**
Forgive us, O God, for carelessness of thought
and deed: for sometimes so easily forgetting the good
things we had hoped to do. Help us to remember them
now, and to make a new beginning with another week:
A new beginning of friendliness for people we could
help—people who are carrying loads heavier than
ours, and doing it bravely and quietly;
A new beginning in sensitiveness to the needs and suffering of this chaotic world, a sensitiveness that will
not let us take for granted the good things we have;
A sensitiveness that will not accept the sacrifice of others,
without giving the warmth of ready affection in
return;
A sensitiveness that will make us considerate of those
who serve us in the humblest ways;
A sensitiveness that will make us ready to share what
we have with men and women and children about
whom we know perhaps little save that they are in
need.
Help us, O Lord, to make indeed a new beginning in a

deepened sense of responsibility for the plan and use of our own days and years and lives. *Amen*

232 THE VALUE OF CHRISTIAN MEETINGS

O God, grant that in our meetings we may always be reverent without stiffness, and serious without being solemn. Give us all a sense of responsibility for the success of the meetings. May we always expect much from them and do all we can to enrich them.

Often we think that our humble meetings, with few present, and often without a specially good topic and with poor attention, mean little, and we sometimes wonder whether we should continue them. Help us, we beseech thee, to see what they may mean to us in the future, and how valuable the training is. May we keep in mind all those who have testified to what they owe to just such meetings as ours. Such meetings have built the foundation of character and faith and have helped in building famous careers.

Help us to work in our own group for the attainment of such high results, that we may have a part in training those who in the years to come will speak and lead for Christ in the various walks of life. In Jesus' name we ask it. *Amen*

233 THREE ARROW PRAYERS

We thank thee, O God, for the poetry of movement: for a bird on the wing, a hare at the run; for a train thundering through the night; for a yacht with spread of sail; for a man running and a child dancing. *Amen*

Lord, take my lips and speak through them, take my mind and think through it, take my heart and set it on fire. *Amen*

O Lord, let us not live to be useless: for the sake of Jesus Christ our Lord. *Amen*

[207]

234 FOR MODESTY

Grant unto us, O Lord, the gift of modesty. When we speak, teach us to give our opinions quietly and sincerely. When we do well in work or play, give us a sense of proportion, that we be neither unduly elated nor foolishly self-depreciatory. Help us in success to realize what we owe to thee and to the efforts of others; in failure, to avoid dejection; and in all ways to be simple and natural, quiet in manner, and lowly in thought: through Christ. *Amen*

235 FOR SELF-CONVICTED WRONGDOERS

O Lord God, our judge and our hope, we remember those whose sin has found them out and has come home to them in sure and secret ways, which no man knoweth but their own heart alone; those who had gone with the fools and knew not that the long ways of thy judgment are in the great deep. We remember them —whom thou hast never forgotten. Accept the amendment of their lives, their silent penitence, their secret pain and prayer; and bring them forth unto the light of forgiveness by the one saving sorrow of thy Son upon his cross. *Amen*

236 FOR ALL WHO ARE DOUBTFUL

Almighty God, we pray for all who, in these days of unsettlement and growing knowledge and changing opinion, are troubled by questioning and doubt. Inspire them with that loyalty of soul to which the things essential to health and peace of life are ever clear. Help us also to put away all such unprofitable and merely curious questionings as would mislead, or hinder us in the practice of those duties which thou requirest of us; and suffer us not to be led astray by vain desires and vain knowledge. What we need to know, teach us; what we cannot know make us content to leave unknown, and to wait patiently on thee till the shadows flee away. *Amen*

237 FOR ANYONE DESPONDENT

Comfort, we beseech thee, most gracious God, this thy servant, cast down and faint of heart amidst the sorrows and difficulties of the world; and grant that by the power of thy Holy Spirit *he* may be enabled to go upon *his* way rejoicing, and give thee continual thanks for thy sustaining providence. *Amen*

238 COURTESY FOR THOSE AMONG WHOM WE LIVE

Accompany me today, O Spirit invisible, in all my goings, but stay with me also when I am in my own house and among those with whom I live. Forbid that I should fail to show to those nearest me the sympathy and consideration which thy grace enables me to show to others with whom I have to do. Forbid that I should refuse to my own household the courtesy and politeness which I think proper to show to strangers. Let charity today begin at home. *Amen*

239 ON RECOGNIZING GOD

O God, it cannot be that thou hast created what thou canst not govern, yet we have been strangely willful and rebellious. We have wrestled all night with one who would overcome us, and then in the morning light we have seen thy face and learned thy name. Surely thou wilt not leave us because we fought against thee: we did not know with whom we strove. Like calm after storm, rest after battle, hope after fear, O come. *Amen*

240 FOR GROWTH WITH THE PASSING YEARS

Almighty and most merciful Father, who hast continued our life from year to year; grant that by longer life we may become less desirous of temporal pleasures and more careful of eternal happiness. So teach us to number our days that our minds may be more withdrawn from vanity and folly, more enlightened with the knowledge of thy will, and more invigorated with power to obey it, for the sake of Jesus Christ our Lord. *Amen*

For a Retreat or Prayer Group

241 O Lord Jesus Christ, who didst say to thy disciples, Come ye apart and rest awhile, grant, we beseech thee, to thy servants now gathered together so to seek thee, whom our souls desire to love, that we may both find thee and be found of thee; and grant such love and such wisdom to accompany the words that shall be spoken in thy name, that they may not fall to the ground, but may be helpful in leading us onward to thy perfect service: who livest and reignest, God for ever and ever. *Amen*

242 Almighty Father, known in our silence and entreated in our hunger for thee, nourish us now with the common bread of thy grace. Shape with thy hands the life of this quiet company, that it may be Christ's own life in our day. Bestow thy serenity and clean strength on each friend whom we now present before thee. . . . Grant us honest work and steadfast friendship in Christ; deepen, O God, thy intention for our life in thee, through Christ our Lord. *Amen*

243 O Father, we are gathered together, a company unknown fully to one another, yet each known to thee. Some cannot think what has brought them hither: old-time custom, unconscious habit, something in the evening sky, a desolation in the heart; knowing not that it was thyself who callest everywhere and movest in all. Some of us are conscious only of our ignorance, aware of the hopeless poverty and confusion of our thoughts. Help us to understand that this is because in the secret places of the mind we touch the wisdom of thy mighty mind and overhear thy glorious thoughts. Some of us are saddened and perplexed by the ugliness and misery around us. Help us to understand that this is because we have seen the holy city descending out of heaven. Some of us are in despair because of unworthiness and sin. Grant us to know that only in thy light could these shadows be discerned.

As stars come out when the sun goes down, strange music sounds when the quiet of evening comes, and voices are heard in the silence which were drowned in the noise of the day, so let us be silent now until thy presence grows more real and we find both doubt and desire but heralds of thy drawing nigh. *Amen*

244 O God our Father, who hast put thy Spirit in men's hearts from days of old, who hast manifested thyself in the lives of men and women who have greatly lived and nobly died, endue us in this hour with some little measure of insight and of understanding. As we draw apart for these short moments, grant us a new perspective on the hurrying events of our crowded hours. Free us from petty anxiety and foolish fears, that we may have power to see the deeper issues of our time, and strength to meet with courageous hearts the obligations which they lay upon us. *Amen*

245 God of compassion, if anyone has come to this place troubled in spirit, depressed and apprehensive, expecting to go away as he came, with the same haunting heaviness of heart; if anyone is deeply wounded of soul, hardly daring to hope that anything can afford him the relief he seeks, so borne down by the ill that life can do that he is half afraid to pray: O God, surprise him, we beseech thee, by the graciousness of thy help; and enable him to take from thy bounty as ungrudgingly as thou givest, that he may leave here his sorrow and take a song away. We ask in the name of Jesus. *Amen*

246 O God our Father, whose blessed Son Jesus Christ did ofttimes forsake the haunts of men and seek some solitary place apart in which to pray; help us, too, in calm and quiet, to find thee very near to us in our prayers, so that when we return once more to the haste and tumult of our crowded life we may, like him, feel thy presence ever with us. *Amen*

247 Blessed God, we have looked into the worn faces of men, into the eyes of those who love us, and now we look for the face of the Son of Man that we may rest. We have seen an end of all perfection; show to us now the glory of the cross, where failure becomes victory, and the bitterness of sin dissolves in tears of penitence. Call us from all that distracts; gather us into the quiet of thy love; meet with us, O Father, for we seek thy face. *Amen*

248 God of all grace, grant unto us thy peace that passes understanding, that the quietness which comes from friendliness with man and true divine friendship

with thee may possess our souls; that we, withdrawn
awhile from the turmoil of the world, may gather the
strength that we have lost and, established and strengthened by thy grace, pass on through all the troubles of
this earthly life, in Christ. *Amen*

Grace at Meals

249   For this day and thy love and this food we thank thee, for Jesus' sake. *Amen*

O God, we thank thee for this food: as we live by thy bounty, may we live continually to thy praise. *Amen*

O Lord, bless this food to our use and us to thy service; for Christ's sake we ask it. *Amen*

For food to nourish our bodies, O God, and friends to cheer our souls, we give thee thanks. *Amen*

Some hae meat and canna eat,
And some would eat that want it:
But we hae meat, and we can eat,
So the good Lord be thankit. *Amen*

Benedictus benedicat. Amen (May the blessed One bless.)

O Lord, give us grateful hearts, and make us mindful of the wants of others, in Christ. *Amen*

For these and all thy gifts, O God, make us truly thankful, through Christ. *Amen*

The Lord bless this food for our use and us in his service, and help us to remember the needs of others, for Christ's sake. *Amen*

Gracious God, may the food which we are about to receive strengthen our bodies and may thy Holy Spirit strengthen and refresh our souls, through Jesus Christ. *Amen*

Thou hast given so much to us, give one thing more: a grateful heart, for Christ's sake. *Amen*

For Special Points in Worship

250   CALLS TO WORSHIP OR TO PRAYER

They that wait upon the Lord shall renew their strength; they shall mount up with wings as eagles; they shall run, and not be weary; they shall walk, and not faint.

The Lord is in his holy temple: let all the earth keep silence before him.

Seek ye the Lord while he may be found; call ye upon him while he is near. The Lord is nigh unto all them that call upon him, to all that call upon him in truth.

Come ye, and let us go up unto the mountains of the Lord, to the house of the Lord our God; and he will teach us of his ways, and we will walk in his paths.

The hour cometh, and now is, when the true worshipers shall worship the Father in spirit and in truth: for the Father seeketh such to worship him. God is spirit, and they that worship him must worship him in spirit and in truth.

O bless the Lord, ye people, and make the voice of his praise to be heard; who holdeth our soul in life, and suffereth not our feet to be moved.

Acquaint now thyself with God, and be at peace; thereby good shall come unto thee. Yea, the Almighty shall be thy defense. For then shalt thou have delight in the Almighty, and shalt lift up thy face unto God.

Come, let us return unto the Lord, for he will heal us. His going forth is prepared as the morning; and he shall come unto us as the rain, as the latter and former rain unto the earth.

O ye servants of the Lord, praise the name of the Lord: from the rising of the sun unto the going down of the same, the Lord's name is to be praised.

251 **THE OFFERING**
Remember the words of the Lord Jesus, how he said, It is more blessed to give than to receive.

All things come of thee, O Lord, and of thine own have we given thee.

Let your light so shine before men, that they may see your good works, and glorify your Father who is in heaven.

Not every one that saith unto me, Lord, Lord, shall enter into the kingdom of heaven; but he that doeth the will of my Father who is in heaven.

To do good, and to distribute, forget not; for with such sacrifices God is well pleased.

And the King shall answer and say unto them, Verily I say unto you, Inasmuch as ye have done it unto one of the least of these my brethren, ye have done it unto me.

252 **THE BENEDICTION**
The grace of the Lord Jesus Christ, and the love of God, and the fellowship of the Holy Spirit be with us all. *Amen*

The Lord bless us and keep us.
The Lord make his face to shine upon us, and be gracious unto us.
The Lord lift up his countenance upon us and give us peace. Now, and for evermore. *Amen*

The peace of God, which passes all understanding, keep your hearts and minds, through Jesus Christ our Lord. *Amen*

Now unto him that is able to keep us from falling, and to present us faultless before the presence of his glory with exceeding joy; to the only wise God our Savior, be glory and majesty, dominion and power, both now and ever. *Amen*

Now unto him who is able to do exceeding abundantly above all that we ask or think, according to the power that worketh in us; unto him be glory in the Church by Christ Jesus throughout all ages, world without end. *Amen*

Now the God of peace, who brought again from the dead our Lord Jesus Christ, that great shepherd of the sheep, through the blood of the everlasting covenant, make us perfect in every good work to do his will, working in us that which is well-pleasing in his sight, through Jesus Christ; to whom be glory for ever and ever. *Amen*

PART V. APPENDIX

Sources and Background

How This Prayerbook Came to Be

The several notable manuals of devotion published by the British Student Christian Movement, like various books by individual compilers and writers, have for decades suggested to students that a prayerbook should be prepared by a group representing the main stream of Christian student life in America.

As this request came to Haddam House (which is described on one of the first pages of this volume), a careful searching out was made of the need and specifications for such a volume. An editorial committee was chosen after this study, with a real effort to draw upon all the main traditions which go to make up the student Christian movement in this country. After two years of research and correspondence, with consultation of the great wealth of resources available, the book was the result of narrowing-down and excision, rather than of merely "gathering" prayers which students have found meaningful.

Special interest led the committee to trace down sources of prayers as completely as possible, one handicap being the fact that many books of prayers give no attribution of authorship. Yet it was the decision of the group that attribution not be made at the close of each prayer, because this often distracts attention from the prayer itself. Thus the best known source of each prayer is given in the listing below. If readers detect inaccuracies, the committee will be grateful to know of them. Because this prayerbook is conceived as a fresh contemporary manual, many prayers (except those familiar by long usage) have been slightly altered or even considerably edited, to speak more directly to this generation. All such changes have been indicated below.

The committee owes a debt of gratitude to the publishers whose names are given with the various books listed: they have been gracious indeed in permitting the use of materials as noted.

Membership of the committee, chosen in consultation with executives of the united student work in this country, has included representation of five major communions and many areas of student concern. Dozens of student leaders have been consulted, and the whole of the manuscript has been scrutinized by a number of advisers. Of the committee itself, John Oliver Nelson has been chairman, the other members being John Deschner, Robert C. Dodds, William W. McKee, Robert Rodenmayer, John W. Vannorsdall, Harold H. Viehman, Frederick Wentz, and Winnifred Wygal. Special help has been given also by Mary Helen Forsberg, Raymond S. Grant, Jr., Harold B. Ingalls, Harry Edmund Smith, and Helen Turnbull, as well as by members of the Haddam House editorial board. James Rietmulder at Association Press has accommodated the committee in numberless ways.

Attributions

Books for which the full title is once given are thereafter noted only by the name of their author or by initials. An asterisk (*) means that the material has been abridged or edited. Prayers marked "New here" and not otherwise attributed are written by the chairman of the committee. The number of the prayer is given here at the left, and sources are listed in order for the various sections under each prayer number.

1. (KPG) *The Kingdom, the Power, and the Glory* (Oxford University Press, New York, 1933), p. 77 *
   Elmore McNeill McKEE, *Communion with God* (Long and Smith, New York, 1932), p. 162 *
   Walter RAUSCHENBUSCH, *Prayers of the Social Awakening* (original title: *For God and the People*)
   (Pilgrim Press, Boston, 1909), p. 47 *
   McKee, p. 39, quoting John Hunter

2. Rauschenbusch, p. 33

   Charles H. BRENT, *Things That Matter* (Harper, New York, 1932), p. 63

   John BAILLIE, *A Diary of Private Prayer* (Scribner, New York, 1936), p. 11

   Francis G. PEABODY, *Prayers for Various Occasions and Needs* (Houghton Mifflin, Boston, 1930), pp. 7-8

3. Daybreak Office of the Eastern Church (3rd century), in McKee, p. 16

   (CPAA) Selina F. FOX, ed., *A Chain of Prayer Across the Ages* (Dutton, New York, 1943), p. 172,* quoting Lancelot Andrewes

   (PNAO) *Prayers New and Old*, booklet of the Forward Movement, Cincinnati, p. 41

   McKee, p. 160 *

   (SP) *Student Prayer* (SCM Press, London, 1950), p. 159, quoting Ignatius Loyola

4. Morgan P. NOYES, *Prayers for Services* (Scribner, New York, 1934), p. 58, quoting James Martineau

   Wade Crawford BARCLAY, *Challenge and Power* (Abingdon, Nashville, 1936), p. 28

   Ernest F. Tittle, in Barclay, p. 178

   Anonymous, 16th century

5. McKee, p. 159 *

   Baillie, p. 29

   McKee, p. 176 *

6. Sarum Primer (1558), in SP, p. 159

   McKee, p. 125

   Rauschenbusch, p. 35

   (BCP) *Book of Common Prayer*, Protestant Episcopal Church, here quoting Gelasian Sacramentary (8th century), p. 31

7. (HFW) *Hymns for Worship* (Association Press, New York, 1939), here quoting Mozarabic Sacramentary (5th century), p. 216

   Walter R. BOWIE, *Lift Up Your Hearts* (Macmillan, New York, 1940), p. 11

   McKee, p. 136 *

8. PNAO, p. 28
   Baillie, p. 111
   KPG, p. 79 *
   David E. ADAMS, *A Little Book of College Prayers*
      (Unity Press, Holyoke, 1944), p. 17 *
   Peabody, p. 7 *

9. Peabody, p. 3
   Bishop Hornby, in CPAA, p. 154
   James Martineau, in McKee, p. 29
   PNAO, p. 44

10. Bowie, p. 19
    Samuel JOHNSON, *Doctor Johnson's Prayers* (Stan-
       ford University Press, 1945), p. 8 *
    Saint Anselm (11th century)
    Joseph B. BERNARDIN, *Prayers for Schools and
       Colleges* (Morehouse, New York, 1933), p. 88
    PNAO, p. 28

11. John DOBERSTEIN, *Prayers for Students* (Muhlen-
       berg Press, Philadelphia, 1951), here quoting Alec
       Petterson, p. 92
    McKee, p. 127
    Uppingham Prayer Book, in McKee, p. 17
    PNAO, p. 4
    Bishop Westcott, in David R. PORTER, *Enrichment
       of Prayer* (Association Press, New York, 1918),
       p. 176

12. Samuel McComb, in Noyes, p. 41
    CPAA (based on Col. 3:1-3 and Psalm 14), p. 9
    McKee, p. 61
    McKee, p. 128

13. McKee, p. 186
    (BPS) *Book of Prayer for Students* (SCM Press,
       London, 1915), p. 29 *
    Peabody, p. 22 (adapted by Willard Sperry)

14. Adams, p. 25 *
    BCP, p. 31
    Rauschenbusch, p. 32 *
    Lancelot Andrewes, in SP, p. 141

15. BCP, p. 594
    McKee, p. 185
    Robert Louis Stevenson, in McKee, p. 52
    Reinhold Niebuhr, in SP, p. 181

16. McKee, p. 134
    Abigail A. JOHNSON, ed., *Prayers for Young People* (Westminster Press, Philadelphia, 1947), p. 95
    Thomas Aquinas (13th century), in SP, p. 151
    Mark 9:24

17. Brent, p. 5
    PNAO, p. 47
    Student Conference, Blue Ridge, N.C., 1938
    McKee, p. 184

18. From Isaiah 30:15 and Psalm 46:10
    Baillie, p. 79
    McKee, p. 156 *
    (PAAM) Mary W. TILESTON, ed., *Prayers Ancient and Modern* (Little, Brown, Boston, 1927), p. 89

19. McKee, p. 135 *
    Baillie, p. 125 *
    Rauschenbusch, p. 31 *

20. Gelasian Sacramentary, in Noyes, p. 104
    PNAO, p. 40
    KPG, p. 15
    Ralph M. Harper, in McKee, p. 37 *
    Psalm 141:2

21. William Bright, in Noyes, p. 36
    Bernardin, p. 59
    McKee, p. 158 *
    Bowie, p. 33 *

22. Based on Acts 17:28 and Romans 12:1-2, in SP, p. 160
    McKee, p. 184
    Baillie, p. 23
    Lohe (19th century), in SP, 139 *

23. Rauschenbusch, p. 28*
    Source unknown
    SP, p. 170

24. Rauschenbusch, p. 34 *
    William H. Spence, in Barclay, p. 172 *
    Arthur Moor, adapted in McKee, p. 128.

25. Rauschenbusch, p. 27 *
    (PD) Lancelot ANDREWES, *Private Devotions*
    (1675) (Abingdon, Nashville, 1950), p. 9
    Adams, p. 9 *
    W. A. Visser 't Hooft, at Student Volunteer Move-
    ment General Council, Oberlin, 1936

26. McKee, p. 131 *
    John HUNTER, *Devotional Services* (Dent, London,
    1901), p. 303 *
    Adams, p. 32 *
    KPG, p. 8

27. CPAA, p. 83
    McKee, p. 162 *
    William DeWitt Hyde in McKee, p. 36
    Adams, p. 7

28. KPG, p. 78
    McKee, p. 144 *
    John Hunter, in Noyes, p. 49 *
    Baillie, p. 63
    Christina G. Rossetti, in PNAO, p. 5

29. (BPYP) Richard K. MORTON, *A Book of Prayers
    for Young People* (Abingdon, 1935), p. 69 *
    (EP) *Everyday Prayers* (SCM Press, London, 19?),
    here quoting H. Bisseker, p. 67 *
    BCP, p. 92
    George Adam Smith, in SP, p. 173
    Thomas à Kempis, in SP, p. 173 *

30. Baillie, p. 57 *
    PD, p. 71
    New here
    St. Francis' Canticle to the Sun (13th century)
    New here

31. New here
    (LCSB) *Lutheran Common Service Book* (United
    Lutheran Church, 1918), p. 114
    Rauschenbusch, p. 101 *
    A. C. Fraser, in SP, p. 174

[226]

32. SP, pp. 19, 26
    BCP, p. 206

33. PNAO, p. 36
    Methodist Orders of Worship (Methodist Book Con-
        cern, 1935), p. 504
    Baillie, p. 67
    George Dawson, in PAAM, p. 319 *
    Roman Breviary, in PAAM, p. 8

34. Willard L. SPERRY, *Prayers for Private Devotions
        in War-Time* (Harper, New York, 1943), quoting
        John Austin, p. 1 *
    George Dawson, in PAAM, p. 341 *
    Augustine, adapted in Sperry, p. 3
    McKee, p. 120 *
    Baillie, p. 25

35. Wilton Rix (after Luther), SP, p. 115
    John Wallace Suter, in Doberstein, p. 69
    Lauchlan MacLean WATT, *Prayers for Public Wor-
        ship* (Allenson, London, n.d.), p. 147 *
    John S. HOYLAND, *A Book of Prayers for Youth*
        British title: *A Book of Prayers Written for Use in
        an Indian College* (Association Press, New York,
        1939), p. 116 *
    Baillie, p. 49
    PNAO, p. 55

36. New here
    Christina G. Rossetti, in PAAM, p. 159
    Dean Vaughan, in Sperry, p. 42
    LCSB, p. 56 *
    New here
    New here
    New here

37. KPG, p. 4
    KPG, p. 23
    New here
    R. Ambrose REEVES, *A Quiet Room* (Harper, New
        York, 1928), p. 81
    KPG, p. 22
    Baillie, p. 113

[227]

38. (BCW) Presbyterian *Book of Common Worship* (Westminster Press, 1932), here quoting Henry Van Dyke, p. 166
    SP, p. 190
    PNAO, p. 32
    LCSB
    New here, suggested by PNAO, p. 58

39. Thomas Wilson, in Sperry, p. 42
    Reeves, p. 47 *
    Baillie, p. 107
    KPG, pp. 55-56
    New here
    W. E. Orchard, in Noyes, p. 63 *

40. PNAO, p. 51
    Reeves, p. 38 *
    KPG, p. 80
    Gelasian Sacramentary, Noyes, p. 104
    John Hunter, in McKee, p. 25 *
    W. E. Orchard, in Noyes, p. 42
    KPG, revised by McKee, p. 54 *

41. BPS, pp. 66-67
    Albert Parker Fitch, in Noyes, p. 75 *
    New here
    J. H. Jowett, in EP, p. 42
    New here
    McKee, p. 191

42. John Donne, in Sperry, p. 38
    Rauschenbusch, p. 126 *
    New here
    Baillie, p. 103 *
    Bernardin, p. 77

43. BCP, p. 90

44. Sperry (A Harvard chapel litany)

45. New here

46. New here

47. World's Student Christian Federation Call to Prayer (*Intercollegian*, Jan. 1952)

48. New here

49. Rayborn L. Zerby (*Intercollegian*, Sept. 1945)

50. McKee, p. 133 *

51. Hayward, Percy (*Intercollegian*, Feb. 1946)

52. Thomas à Kempis, in Noyes, p. 150

53. SP, p. 183

54. King's College, Cambridge, in SP, p. 182

55. BPYP, p. 98 *

56. Johnson, p. 5

57. PNAO, p. 79

58. Sperry, p. 31

59. Sperry, p. 37

60. BPS, p. 127

61. BPS, p. 72

62. SP, p. 157

63. Baillie, p. 133

64. SP, p. 122

65. F. H. Sill, in McKee, p. 70

66. Jack FINEGAN, *Book of Student Prayers* (Association Press, New York, 1946), No. 12

67. SP, p. 183

68. SP, p. 51

69. SP, pp. 63-64

70. New here
    New here
    Finegan, No. 209
    G. M. Paterson, in Doberstein, p. 91 *

71. New here

72. Bernardin, p. 95

73. New here

74. Bernardin, p. 47
    S. P. T. Prideaux, in SP, p. 184
    Bowie, p. 64

75. New here
    Rauschenbusch, p. 87 *
    Morton, p. 13

76. McKee, p. 192 *
    Finegan, No. 213

77. New here

78. New here

79. New here

80. New here

81. New here

82. New here

83. New here

84. New here

85. New here

86. New here

87. New here

88. SP, p. 185
    Bernardin, p. 63
    PNAO, p. 4
    David E. ADAMS, *A Little Book of College Prayers*
    (Unity Press, Holyoke, Mass., 1944), p. 35 *

89. *Family Prayer Book of Church of Ireland*, in McKee,
    p. 63 *
    Bernardin, pp. 17-18

90. SP, p. 183

91. Prayers of World-Wide Church, in SP, p. 172
    BPS, p. 161

92. New here

93. New here

94. New here

95. New here

96. New here

97. New here

98. Based on BPS, p. 39

99. New here

100. New here

101. Based on KPG, p. 3

102. Reinhold Niebuhr, in HFW, p. 224 *

103. New here

104. SP, pp. 74-76

105. SP, pp. 76-78

106. J. H. Jowett, in Sperry, p. 15
New here
J. H. Jowett, in EP, p. 67
BPS, p. 74
John Austin, in Sperry, p. 15

107. Hoyland, p. 96

108. McKee, pp. 152, 127, 187 *
SP, pp. 81-82 *
Sperry (A Harvard chapel litany)
Francis G. Peabody, in Noyes, p. 46 *
Adams, p. 15
New here

109. BPYP, p. 102 *
BPS, p. 165
BPYP, p. 37
BPS, p. 73 *

110. New here
SP, p. 59 *
G. W. Briggs, in SP, p. 122

111. New here
McKee, p. 69
Rauschenbusch, p. 69 *

112. SP, p. 182
Rauschenbusch, pp. 63-64 *
BPYP, p. 103 *

113. New here
Sperry (A Harvard chapel litany)
Sperry, p. 28
H. J. Wetherspoon, in SP, p. 171 *

114. New here
Based on SP., p. 55 *
New here

115. New here
     BPS, p. 53 *
     Rauschenbusch, p. 83 *

116. New here
     Based on SP, pp. 56-60
     New here

117. New here
     BPYP, p. 30 *
     New here
     New here

118. New here
     Mornay Williams, in Rauschenbusch, p. 71 *
     SP, p. 184 *
     Rauschenbusch, p. 75 *

119. New here
     Rauschenbusch, p. 57 *
     James MYERS, *Prayers, Personal and Social* (Federal Council, New York, 1943), p. 35 *
     New here

120. New here
     Sperry, p. 29
     New here
     Rauschenbusch, p. 77 *

121. New here
     Sperry, p. 22
     New here

122. Sperry (A Harvard chapel litany *)
     New here
     Based on SP, p. 58

123. New here
     BPS, p. 153 *
     Based on SP, p. 62

124. New here
     Rauschenbusch, p. 79 *
     Based on SP, p. 53

125. HFW, p. 224
     Myers, p. 33

126. New here

127. BPS, p. 36 *
    BPYP, p. 41 *

128. BPS, p. 16 *

129. KPG, p. 31

130. Rauschenbusch, p. 119 *

131. PNAO, p. 60

132. P. T. FORSYTH, *Intercessory Services* (Heywood, London, 1896), Gelasian Sacramentary revised, p. 21

133. *Venite Adoremus I* (Service of the Church of Sweden, from Didache, 2nd century), p. 49

134. McKee, p. 166 *

135. Franciscan Breviary (13th century), in SP, p. 165

136. Forsyth, p. 8

137. BPS, p. 143 *

138. Forsyth, p. 14

139. Hunter, p. 263 *

140. George STEWART, *A Face to the Sky: a Book of Prayers* (Association Press, New York, 1940), p. 94

141. BPYP, pp. 11-12 *

142. BPS, p. 77

143. Liturgy of St. James (2nd century), BPS, p. 142 *

144. Federal Council Bulletin, 1940, in SP, p. 167 *

145. *Prayers for All Occasions* (The Forward Movement, Cincinnati, n.d.), p. 42 *

146. BPS, p. 145

147. New here, by Tracey Jones

148. KPG, pp. 19-21 *

149. BPS, p. 48

150. BPS, p. 161 *

151. Finegan, No. 9

152. H. Bisseker, in EP, p. 69 *

153. Bowie, p. 41

154. BPYP, p. 54 *

155. Bowie, p. 42

156. Bowie, p. 43

157. Bowie, pp. 43-44

158. Bowie, p. 44

159. John HUNTER, *Devotional Services* (Dent, London, 1901), p. 247

160. BPYP, p. 60 *

161. Hunter, p. 247 *

162. Hunter, p. 249

163. Louis F. Benson and Henry Van Dyke, in BCW, pp. 172-173 *

164. Hunter, p. 248

165. Hunter, p. 225 *
Bowie, p. 48

166. Hunter, p. 227

167. New here
New here

168. New here

169. *Lutheran Hymnal* (Concordia Publishing House, St. Louis, Mo., 1941), p. 4
KPG, p. 73
SP, pp. 87-88

170. Thomas Aquinas, in SP, p. 89
Gregorian Sacramentary, in BCP, p. 114

171. Henry Van Dyke, in BCW, p. 203
John Henry Newman, in BCW, p. 100
BPYP, p. 47 *
Bowie, p. 25
Prayers for All Occasions, p. 26 *
Hoyland, p. 28 *

172. BCW, p. 103 *
Hoyland, p. 29 *

173. BPS, p. 115 *

174. Henry Van Dyke in BCW, p. 168 *

175. Reinhold Niebuhr, in Noyes, p. 64

[234]

176. Bishop Brooke F. Westcott, 19th century, in BPS, p. 157
177. BPS, p. 158 *
178. KPG, p. 33 *
    New here
179. New here—suggested by Reeves, pp. 35-36
180. Rauschenbusch, p. 97 *
181. KPG, pp. 54-55 *
182. Forsyth, p. 17
    S. Ralph HARLOW, *Prayers for Times Like These* (Association Press, New York, 1942), p. 20 *
    McKee, p. 149 *
183. William Temple, in Doberstein, p. 66
    New here
    HFW, p. 233, quoting here Book of Christian Prayer, 1578
184. Bowie, p. 97
185. Forsyth, p. 18 *
186. Rauschenbusch, p. 59 *
187. Percy R. Hayward, in *Intercollegian*, Feb., 1946
188. BPS, p. 152 *
189. Forsyth, p. 26 *
190. New here
191. The Challenge, in EP, p. 75 *
192. New here
193. Bowie, p. 94
194. BPS, p. 11 *
195. W. E. ORCHARD, *The Temple* (Dutton, New York, Seventh Edition, 1946), p. 162
196. *Intercollegian*, April, 1948
197. Based on Adams, p. 24
198. Rauschenbush, p. 117 *
199. *Prayers for All Occasions*, p. 35
200. McKee, p. 189

201. Harlow, p. 26 *

202. New here

203. Rauschenbusch, p. 100 *

204. LBCP, p. 20

205. Bowie, p. 37

206. New here. Based on "A Bill of Human Rights" (United Nations, 1951)

207. McKee, p. 124 *
    LBCP, p. 30
    Reinhold Niebuhr (verified by the author)

208. KPG, p. 66

209. KPG, pp. 15, 71

210. Hunter, p. 111 *

211. Ted Hume, in *Intercollegian*, June, 1945 *

212. KPG, p. 13

213. Bowie, p. 102 *

214. BCP, p. 19

215. BCP, p. 6

216. Gregorian Sacramentary (7th century)

217. Leonine Sacramentary (5th century)

218. William Bright, in Noyes, p. 36

219. Hunter, p. 52 *

220. Francis of Assisi, in SP, p. 146

221. Gelasian Sacramentary (8th century), in BCP, p. 174

222. Gregorian Sacramentary (8th century), in BCP, p. 49

223. Gelasian Sacramentary (8th century), in BCP, p. 17

224. Chrysostom, in BCP, p. 20

225. Gelasian Sacramentary (8th century), in BCP, p. 31

226. BCP, p. 124, quoting Prayerbook of 1549

227. KPG, p. 70

228. Hoyland, p. 82

229. Baillie, p. 103

230. CPAA, p. 94

231. LBCP, p. 34

232. BPYP, p. 78

233. Camp Prayer, in EP, p. 29.
W. H. H. Aitken, in PAAM, p. 336
John Wesley, in EP, p. 35

234. Bernardin, p. 74 *

235. Forsyth, p. 12 *

236. Hunter, p. 266 *

237. BCP, p. 316

238. Baillie, p. 89

239. Orchard, p. 24 *

240. Samuel Johnson, in BCW, p. 169 *

241. R. M. Benson, in BPS, p. 163

242. The Kirkridge Discipline *

243. Orchard, p. 98 *

244. LBCP, p. 36

245. A. W. Palmer, *Aids to Worship* (Macmillan, New York, 1944), p. 103 *

246. McKee, p. 7 *

247. Orchard, p. 100 *

248. George Dawson, in Noyes, p. 38 *

249. Robert Burns *
The Tent and Altar, 1847, in EP, p. 107
George Herbert, in EP, p. 107

250. Isaiah 40:31; Habakkuk 2:20; Isaiah 55:6 and Psalm 145:18; Isaiah 2:3; John 4:23-24; Psalm 66:8-9; Job 22:21, 26; Hosea 6:1, 3; Psalm 113:1, 3

251. Acts 20:35; I Chronicles 29:14; Matthew 5:16; Matthew 7:21; Hebrews 13:16; Matthew 25:40

252. II Corinthians 13:14; Numbers 6:24-26; Philippians 4-7; Jude 24-25; Ephesians 3:20-21; Hebrews 13:20-21

Haddam House Books

BEYOND THIS DARKNESS, *Roger L. Shinn*

CHRISTIAN FAITH AND MY JOB, *Alexander Miller*

PRIMER FOR PROTESTANTS, *James Hastings Nichols*

PREFACE TO ETHICAL LIVING, *Robert E. Fitch*

THE GRAND INQUISITOR, *Fyodor Dostoevsky*

YOUTH ASKS ABOUT RELIGION, *Jack Finegan*

YOUNG LAYMEN—YOUNG CHURCH, *John Oliver Nelson*

THE HUMAN VENTURE IN SEX, LOVE AND MARRIAGE,
Peter A. Bertocci

SCIENCE AND CHRISTIAN FAITH,
Edward LeRoy Long, Jr.

A GOSPEL FOR THE SOCIAL AWAKENING
Walter Rauschenbusch

THE CHRISTIAN IN POLITICS, *Jerry Voorhis*

REDISCOVERING THE BIBLE, *Bernhard W. Anderson*

LIFE'S MEANING, *Henry P. Van Dusen*

THAT ALL MAY BE ONE,
James Edward Lesslie Newbigin

THE QUEST FOR CHRISTIAN UNITY,
Robert S. Bilheimer

THE CHRISTIAN STUDENT AND THE CHURCH,
J. Robert Nelson, Editor

THE CHRISTIAN STUDENT AND THE UNIVERSITY
J. Robert Nelson, Editor

THE CHRISTIAN STUDENT AND THE WORLD STRUGGLE,
J. Robert Nelson, Editor

THE UNFOLDING DRAMA OF THE BIBLE
Bernhard W. Anderson

THE STUDENT PRAYERBOOK,
John Oliver Nelson and Others, Editors

RIVERSIDE POETRY
HOW TO MAKE FRIENDS ABROAD
Robert Root

COMMUNITY OF FAITH, *T. Ralph Morton*

ENCOUNTER WITH REVOLUTION, *M. Richard Shaull*

POLITICS FOR CHRISTIANS, *William Muehl*

THE PARADOXES OF DEMOCRACY,
Kermit Eby and June Greenlief

THE TRAGIC VISION AND THE CHRISTIAN FAITH
Nathan A. Scott, Editor

CONSCIENCE ON CAMPUS, *Waldo Beach*

THE PROPHETIC VOICE IN MODERN FICTION
William R. Mueller

THE RENEWAL OF HOPE, *Howard Clark Kee*

CHRISTIANITY AND COMMUNISM TODAY,
John C. Bennett

NOTES

NOTES

NOTES

NOTES